# 2BRIDES 2BE

*A same-sex guide for the modern bride*

# 2BRIDES 2BE

## 2BE

*A same-sex guide for the modern bride*

## LAURA LEIGH ABBY

A GENUINE ARCHER BOOK

ARCHER/RARE BIRD

453 South Spring Street · Suite 302 · Los Angeles · CA 90013
archerlit.com

FIRST TRADE PAPERBACK ORIGINAL EDITION

Set in Minion
Printed in the United States

Book Design by starling
Illustrations by Cara Lowe

10 9 8 7 6 5 4 3 2 1

Publisher's Cataloging-in-Publication data

Names: Abby, Laura Leigh, author.
Title: 2Brides 2be : a same-sex guide for the modern bride /
Laura Leigh Abby.
Description: Includes bibliographical references. | A Genuine Archer
Book | First Trade Paperback Original Edition | New York, NY;
Los Angeles, CA: Archer/Rare Bird Books, 2017.
Identifiers: ISBN 9781941729175
Subjects: LCSH Wedding—Planning. | Wedding—Equipment and
supplies. | Same-sex marriage. | Lesbian couples. | Etiquette for
lesbians. | BISAC REFERENCE / Weddings.
Classification: LCC HQ745 .A23 2017 | DDC 392.5—dc23

*To my wife Samantha,*
*you are forever my beautiful bride.*

# CONTENTS

# Foreward

by Trish Bendix

**W**OMEN HAVE BEEN MARRYING each other for decades, long before cities, states, and countries deemed their matrimony legal. Whether it was a private ceremony and celebration or a Boston marriage never given its full appreciation from the outside world, love has been kept secret (or ignored by some), but embraced and cherished by those who know it best.

We've seen some great strides for equal marriage in the twenty-first century, and with every positive turn of legislation, more and more couples take the step to sanctify their relationship with weddings of their very own, a publicly commemorated day dedicated to the love of two women who want to be together for the rest of their lives, in sickness and in health, 'til death do they part.

Most of these women have grown up without any kind of idea what this might look like. There have been very few depictions of lesbian weddings in mainstream media or pop culture, and even then, those very-special-episodes don't always illustrate the entirety of the planning process. It's only the vows and the cake-cutting, the first dances and the dresses. There's so much more to worry about, and worry you surely will.

The common guides and how-to's for wedding planning are very heterosexual, and it's not as easy as borrowing the bride-groom aesthetic and adapting for bride-bride.

The secret to having an ideal same-sex wedding is to discard everything you think you know about the nuptials and ceremonies and "yes to the dresses." One of the best things about being a queer woman is that you can rewrite history—you have the chance to create the kind of big day that you haven't even begun to dream about. There aren't any "rules" for you or your partner; no one *has* to perform the expected duties of the groom—there is no groom! There's just you and your spouse-to-be—your wife, should you decide to use the conventional term, and accept it for yourself as well.

It can be overwhelming to start from scratch, though, which is why it's the perfect timing for a collection of helpful suggestions from those who have been through it, from the beginning stages of big ideas to the final execution of the big day. The important thing to remember is that this all began out of the want to be together, and to invite your loved ones to share in that excitement. Forget the expectations you think others might have of you, the ones wedding culture can sometimes perpetuate. (It's a business for many, after all.) Keep your eye on the prize: your legally wedded wife.

As the anxiety builds, the vendor bills stack up, and the RSVPs roll in, center yourself in knowing that women have been doing this without a road map for years, and that the only obligation you have is to yourselves. Every single part of a wedding ceremony and reception is optional, except for you and your chosen partner for life. Finding that person is worth celebrating. It always has been, and always will be.

# Introduction

AFTER A VACATION PROPOSAL in August 2012, I boarded my flight home with a diamond on my finger and wedding magazines in my carry-on. In the weeks that followed, I stayed up late with my laptop open on my comforter and magazines scattered around me. I clicked through wedding blogs and dog-eared pictures of dresses I thought might flatter my frame. Occasionally I awoke my fiancée, Sam, to ask her opinion on floral trends and letterpress. What I saw in the pages and on my screen were women in white gowns and grooms in bespoke suits. Occasionally I'd come across a feature of a same-sex couple, but I had to do some digging to find them. Finally, I gave up. I turned to same-sex wedding publications. I googled "lesbian wedding." The stories and images this search revealed did little to encourage me; I felt unrepresented everywhere I looked.

As I entered the very traditional world of wedding planning I sought inspiration. I yearned for beautiful images of women in love and advice on how to plan a wedding that was both customary and contemporary with the conviction that I would have the wedding of my dreams because I was marrying a woman, not in spite of it. I wanted my wedding to blend tradition with rebellion and focus on the whole of my relationship, not the one aspect that sets us apart. Sam and I were not trying to plan a "lesbian wedding." We were trying to plan *our* wedding: one that reflected us as a couple, a lifetime of love from both friends and family, and our shared hopes for a future of unity.

Loved ones were excited by the details of our wedding plans, but they had questions. As the inquiries grew repetitive, I decided to start a blog. I wrote about the search for the perfect wedding dress and how we chose the elements of our ceremony. I discussed the hardships we faced in changing our names and the logistics of planning a two-bride wedding. I found myself thrust into a position of authority on a subject in which I was clearly no expert—I'd never planned a wedding! The summer before our nuptials I published an essay in the *New York Observer*, "Who Walks Down The Aisle First?" The title was taken from the question I'd been asked most often, that and "are you both wearing dresses?" This was my first realization that it wasn't just my family that was interested in the logistics, the public was curious about wedding planning for same-sex couples as well. So I kept writing. I wanted other women like me to know that we're not alone, that we shouldn't have to feel like aliens invading the world of weddings.

In the past few years, as I've planned a wedding, gotten married, and enjoyed life as a newlywed, I've watched the United States become a nation of marriage equality. The timing feels like kismet. Women who are marrying women no longer have to be the "other." We deserve the same wedding inspiration and practical advice as everyone else.

Over time I have heard from a variety of women who want advice on big issues, like coming out to family, and smaller issues, like how to give a great speech at a lesbian wedding. All of these women are looking for one thing: community. I hope that some day soon lesbian weddings will blend seamlessly into the wedding industry, but for now, we must forge our own path, and I am honored to be your guide. A marriage is a serious commitment. A wedding is a celebration. It's about time the next generation of brides feels the inspiration to plan the wedding of her dreams. You should not have to forfeit romance or whimsy, elegance or grandeur, a rustic vibe or a black-tie affair. I want to help you plan a wedding that is authentic. I want your wedding to be yours. I want you to cherish every milestone, and I want you to know that you are a part of a community that knows the truth: two brides are better than one.

# A TIMELINE OF GAY MARRIAGE AND LESBIAN MILESTONES IN THE UNITED STATES[1]

**May 18, 1970**—A gay couple applies for a marriage license in Minnesota. They are denied all the way up through the Supreme Court.

**1973**—Maryland bans same-sex marriage.

**1974**—Kathy Kozachenko becomes the first openly gay American elected to public office in Michigan.

**1984**—Nation's first domestic partnership law passed in Berkeley, California.

**October 10, 1987**—First mass same-sex wedding takes place at the National Mall in Washington, DC.

**July 1989**—New York State Court of Appeals declares that lesbian or gay couples living together for at least ten years are defined as family.

**1990**—World Health Organization (WHO) removes homosexuality from their list of mental disorders.

**1990**—In Maine, Dale McCormick becomes the first out lesbian elected to the state Senate.

**1991**—The first lesbian kiss on television occurs on an episode of *L.A. Law*.

---

1       Sources: Wikipedia, ProCon.org, GALE Foundation.

**1993**—The first Dyke March is held with twenty thousand women in attendance.

**May 1993**—Hawaii Supreme Court rules in favor of same-sex marriage.

**May 1993**—Hawaii lawmakers pass an amendment banning gay marriage.

**May 1994**—An episode of the popular sitcom *Roseanne* features a lesbian character.

**1994**—Deborah Batts becomes the first openly gay or lesbian federal judge.

**1995**—The District of Columbia Court of Appeals upholds the denial of a license between a same-sex couple.

**1996**—One of the most popular sitcoms of all time, *Friends*, features a lesbian wedding.

**September 21, 1996**—President Clinton signs the Defense of Marriage Act (DOMA), which defines marriage as a union between a man and a woman.

**February 1997**—Ellen DeGeneres comes out.

**1997**—Minnesota bans same-sex marriage.

**1998**—Alaska Supreme Court rules in favor of same-sex marriage.

**1998**—Voters in Alaska and Hawaii define marriage as between one man and one woman.

**1999**—The Supreme Court of Hawaii upholds the state's ban on same-sex marriage.

**1999**—The Vermont Supreme Court rules that excluding same-sex couples from marriage violates the state constitution.

**2000**—Vermont issues the first same-sex unions in the United States.

**2000**—Voters in California and Nebraska define marriage as between one man and one woman.

**2001**—A lesbian couple in the Netherlands become the first same-sex couple to legally marry.

**2002**—Voters in Nevada define marriage as between one man and one woman.

**2003**—The Massachusetts Supreme Court passes a decision granting marriage rights to same-sex couples.

**2004**—Showtime premiers *The L Word*, a television drama focused on the lives of a group of lesbian, bisexual, and transgender friends in Los Angeles.

**2004**—Del Martin and Phyllis Lyon became the first same-sex couple to be legally married in the United States.

**2004**—Marriage licenses are issued to same-sex couples in San Francisco, CA; Sandoval County, NM; New Paltz, NY; Asbury Park, NJ; Multnomah County, OR.

**2004**—Voters in Missouri, Louisiana, Arkansas, Georgia, Kentucky, Michigan, Mississippi, Montana, North Dakota, Ohio, Oklahoma,

Oregon, and Utah approve state constitutional amendments defining marriage as the union of one man and one woman.

**2004**—President Bush calls for a consitutional amendment to define marriage as between one man and one woman.

**2005**—Voters in Kansas and Texas define marriage as between one man and one woman.

**2006**—Voters in Alabama, Colorado, Idaho, South Carolina, South Dakota, Tennessee, Virginia, and Wisconsin define marriage as between one man and one woman.

**2006**—Laurel Hester, a veteran officer in Ocean County, NJ, fights to extend pension benefits to registered domestic partners.

**2008**—New York Governor David Paterson orders state agencies to recognize same-sex marriages from other jurisdictions.

**2008**—The Supreme Court of California overturns the state's ban on same-sex marriage.

**2008**—The year that gay marriage is legalized in California, Ellen DeGeneres marries Portia de Rossi.

**2008**—The Democratic National Convention takes a stance against DOMA and in support of same-sex marriage.

**2008**—The Republican National Convention endorses the Federal Marriage Amendment that protects "traditional marriage" between one man and one woman.

**2008**—Voters in Arizona and Florida define marriage as between one man and one woman.

**2008**—Connecticut legalizes same-sex marriage.

**2008**—Proposition 8 is passed in California, which bans same-sex marriage.

**2009**—Iowa, Maine, Vermont, and New Hampshire legalize same-sex marriage.

**2010**—Washington, DC, legalizes same-sex marriage.

**2010**—Court rules that Proposition 8 is unconstitutional.

**2011**—The Obama Administration announces that they've determined parts of DOMA to be unconstitutional.

**2011**—The military's "Don't Ask Don't Tell" policy is repealed.

**2012**—New York and Washington legalize same-sex marriage.

**2012**—Tammy Baldwin is elected as the first openly gay US Senator.

**2012**—President Barack Obama announces his support for same-sex marriage; he is the first sitting president ever to do so.

**2012**—The first same-sex marriage on a military base takes place in New Jersey.

**2012**—The Democratic National Convention adopts a political platform that supports marriage equality.

**2012**—In *United States v. Windsor*, the Second Circuit Court of Appeals rules section three of the Defense of Marriage Act (DOMA) unconstitutional. Later that year the US Supreme Court agrees to review the case.

**2013**—Maryland, Rhode Island, Delaware, Hawaii, Illinois, and Minnesota legalize same-sex marriage.

**2013**—Supreme Court Justice Ruth Bader Ginsburg becomes the first member of the court to officiate a same-sex marriage.

**2013**—The first Utah marriage licenses are issued to same-sex couples.

**2014**—Same-sex marriage bans are struck down in Alaska, Arizona, Arkansas, Colorado, Indiana, Kentucky, Florida, Idaho, Louisiana, Michigan, Mississippi, Missouri, Montana, Nevada, Oklahoma, Oregon, Pennsylvania, South Carolina, Texas, Utah, Virginia, Wisconsin, and Wyoming.

**2014**—Two Arkansas lesbians are the first same-sex couple to receive a marriage license in the overlapping southern regions of East Dixie and the Bible Belt.

**2015**—Same-sex marriage bans are struck down in Nebraska, South Dakota, and Texas.

**June 26, 2015**—The United States Supreme Court rules in *Obergefell v. Hodges* that because the fundamental right to marry extends to same-sex couples, same-sex marriage bans are unconstitutional under the Fourteenth Amendment. The decision renders same-sex marriage legal throughout the entire United States.

# My 2Bride Beginning

**D**URING MY TEEN YEARS on Long Island I worked at a country club that specialized in waterfront weddings. My uniform included a red bow tie and cummerbund, and through the years I must have poured hundreds of glasses of champagne, popped about a thousand crab cakes into my mouth, and salivated over many, many wedding cakes as the sous chef sliced through the fondant. Too young to really think about what I wanted for my own future wedding, I merely kept in mind the things I didn't want. The list included a DJ as emcee, salmon with dill sauce, and a dry vanilla wedding cake.

One clear autumn evening—I must have been sixteen—I stood just inside the doors of the venue's entrance. I was to greet guests with a tray of flutes, full and sparkling. This was a coveted position because it meant I didn't have to walk around the garden room passing out hors d'oeuvres. One gentleman arrived and caught up with his friends, who immediately asked, "Where's your better half?" His wife was parking the car and this wasn't the first time I'd ever heard the phrase, but something struck me then. I wrote it in my journal when I got home that night: *better half.*

I was a tall teenager, freckle-faced and insecure, so no, I didn't date much. I never even worked up the courage to talk to any of the boys I had crushes on. But on this night I really began to wonder, is there someone out there who will love me, who will make me complete, who will be my better half? *What's he like?* I wondered, and never for a moment did I imagine that *he* might be a *she*.

By my sophomore year of college I was single, in a sorority, and working on my confidence. At the first rush meeting of the year I met Sam, a transfer student from Florida. I immediately disliked her. It seemed to me that we were opposites. She didn't appear to play by the rules; she did whatever she wanted and didn't care what anyone thought of her. I wouldn't have known to admit it at the time, but I cared what everyone thought of me. During the semester that she was pledging I grew closer to Sam, but I never wrote about her in my daily journal entries. When I realized that my feelings for her eclipsed friendship, I wondered two things: *How can I feel this way about someone I barely like?*—and—*Am I gay?*

So many women have been where I was, and, scared of the unknown, or fearful of what friends and family might think, they convince themselves that these feelings are nothing. I admit I tried this method, but I quickly learned that these feelings which so consumed my mind were not nothing, and that ready or not, I needed to explore my feelings for Sam.

It turns out that neither of us was ready. Sam and I tried and failed and tried again to be a couple within our college sorority. In the beginning there were secret kisses, and denials to friends. We snuck around for a while, and I bet that this feels like a familiar feature of many young same-sex relationships. Most of us are raised wanting be somewhere on the special end of the normal spectrum. I wanted to be a little prettier and a little smarter but I didn't want to be unusual. I did not know how to behave as this *other*. The pressure on the relationship back then—when we both knew we were falling for the other but didn't know yet how to think outside of ourselves—nearly annihilated our relationship more than once. Childish things, it feels like now, but familiar things nonetheless: I went to Europe to study abroad for four months, a lifetime when love is on the line. We let past relationships and sexual encounters get in the way of our devotion. A few years into our relationship we even took a few months apart as I sought to find some truth within myself. A question rang through my ears during this time: *are you ready to identify as a lesbian?*

That's the world we live in right? Some of you out there have known yourselves as gay for most of your lives. Others identify as bisexual, and still others swear it's just **this** girl, you love **this** person. Whatever it is, a same-sex couple knows this to be an identifying trait to outsiders. As a young woman, I grappled with what this meant for me. I didn't know for sure if this life I was living was who I really was.

Luckily for me, Sam was patient. I could be *normal,* or I could be with the woman I so achingly loved. Looking back, it seems there was no contest. We are not the perfect couple. We faced years of on-again-off-again, adolescent bullshit. Ours was not a whirlwind romance, or love at first sight. We met at nineteen and grew up together, pushing and pulling each other as we morphed into the women we would become. I am a messy, stubborn, social loudmouth. Sam is organized to a fault, quick to apologize during arguments, and values her alone time (with me and our two Pomeranians, of course). We bicker often and have been known to fight in front of friends, but there's a passion within our relationship that favors our differences.

During our courtship, Sam—the romantic one—planned our dates and surprised me with thoughtful gestures that I pretended to hate but really loved. She invited me to become a part of her family while I was still too scared to introduce her to my own. In a same-sex relationship, patience can be an important element. Sometimes the pace of the relationship is not only dependant on the couple, but on their loved ones as well. Sam let me introduce her as my roommate to extended family, and when we moved together to Los Angeles, I understood why no one at her talent agency knew she had a girlfriend. We reached these milestones on our own time, and that's not to say we didn't face adversity. We hurt each other. We lied to each other. I tried to leave Sam more than once, but each time we came back to each other, incapable of happiness without the other.

Over the years Sam and I learned how to be better people together. I taught Sam how to be honest about her feelings, and she taught me how to love someone more than myself. Over a decade later, I know that Sam, my wife, is as much a part of me as my limbs; I cannot hold her hand without my own, and I could not carry on without her.

As a teenage girl, I imagined a future with a husband, but instead my future brought a wife. I did not expect her but I needed her. It took years for me to realize that I wanted to be a woman with a wife, social norms be damned. Our life together was and is a thing of unique beauty. I could not plan a life worrying about outside noise. Any doubts at this future of having to identify myself as gay were eclipsed by the joy of having Sam as my partner in life. It's okay if it takes you time to realize this. I try not to be too hard on myself when I consider the past. Time's comet-like tail of debris shimmers with perspective. I do not take it lightly that I can remember the moment I met Sam, and though I didn't know it at the time, that flicker of emotion I felt meant that together we would become something extraordinary. This knowledge is a gift, one I've mused on many times over the past decade. On my wedding day, my father escorted me in front of friends and family toward a past, a present, and a promise for the future. I would not let the outside noise disrupt the everlasting tones of our love. I walked toward this truth, and there she was to meet me: my better half.

# PART ONE
## Let's Commence

**W**EDDING PLANNING IS A marriage of huge decisions—*I want to spend my life with you*—and smaller details—*I want peonies in my bouquet.* Faced with planning all of this at once, any woman could morph into a runaway bride. That's why it's important to take the time that you need. That's right, you. I reject the notion that there are rules you must follow. Sure, there are good suggestions and proper etiquette, but the beauty of a two-bride wedding is freedom. Lesbian weddings are still a bit of a novel idea, and from the proposal to the after party, you and your bride-to-be get to do what works best for you.

Still, you must begin somewhere. Go through the following chapters as a couple; or maybe you're planning a surprise proposal and want some early guidance, you'll find that here, too. My hope is that you'll emerge not only with a better idea of how your wedding story is going to read, but you'll also be excited to write it.

### EXPERT TIP

*Stephanie Karvellas-Baynton, Owner & Venue Coordinator at Cedar Lakes Estate*

**What's the first thing you ask new clients?**

*Tell me your story.*

# Who Asks Whom?

IT WAS 2012, AND in the months before we got engaged, Sam developed an addiction to viral proposal videos. Remember those? They were everywhere at the time, and she would watch them and weep. *She would watch people she has never met propose to other people she has never met, and she would be moved to tears.* Occasionally she said, "Babe you have to watch this, it's so cute." If I was bored at that moment, I'd watch, and it often took only thirty seconds before I'd squish up my face and say something along the lines of, "This is so cheesy," or "Kill me," or "This guy is a tool." Seriously, she showed me a proposal once that took place at a CrossFit gym (I mean, I hear those people are really committed) and about a hundred flash mob proposals, to which I always responded, "Do not humiliate me like that. Ever."

Admittedly (and this is not the last time you'll hear this) I am not a romantic. My wife is. I truly believed that we would decide to get engaged when it was the right time, go get some rings, and start wearing them. I thought the idea of a grand proposal—especially between two women—was a little silly. I mean really, why ask if you aren't certain she'll say yes? And if you're certain she'll say yes then just get on with it and plan the wedding. Like my soft-spot for pop music ("Teenage Dream" on repeat, and, yes, I did use some Katy Perry in my own wedding ceremony) I did a one-eighty once Sam proposed. That mushy gushy bullshit was actually thoughtful and moving and, although I already knew that I was this girl's number nine, her romantic proposal made me feel like the absolute luckiest, most-loved woman on the planet. Truly.

So it goes without saying that these days I'm a sucker for a perfect proposal story. Sure, I still have my own opinions about what makes a great proposal, but that's the beauty of proposing: it's about the couple. That's it. Nobody's else's opinion really matters. That means you can plan a proposal around your girlfriend's favorite hobby, sport, food, book—there are no rules. And when it comes to lesbian couples getting engaged, this lack of rules makes for endless possibilities.

### So who asks whom?

This depends on the couple. Some couples decide who is going to do the asking. Then the other one waits impatiently, dropping not-so-subtle hints, while her woman attempts to plan the perfect proposal. Some choose a special day and propose to each other. Still others have one lady just bursting with the absolute *need* to pop the question, no matter how many times the other says, "No rush, babe." I've heard every possible scenario when it comes to lesbians getting engaged, and all these stories I've heard always end with a resounding, "Yes!" My own engagement was of the "no rush, babe" variety. I felt so young (emotionally and physically) and we were coming off of hard times (death and trauma, the two of which were unrelated and therefore added to the "oh shit" behavior that resulted). I knew beyond any doubt that we wanted to spend the rest of our lives together, but the act of getting engaged, all the hullaballoo that followed? Oh God, I simply did not have the energy. Luckily Sam almost never listens to me. She had a plan, she stuck to it, and for that I am grateful every day of my life.

### What about rings?

Two women = two rings, right? Again, not always. Some couples buy rings together and voila! They're both proposal ready. Sometimes one woman proposes with a ring for her beloved, and her own ring comes later. My wife not only had a diamond ring custom-made for me, but she had the same jeweler reset her late mother's diamond for herself, so that as soon as I stopped babbling, "Are you kidding me?" and finally said, "Of course I'll marry you," she handed me her own ring and instructed me to then ask her. A perfectly planned counter-proposal. (I refer to her as a *control freak*, but if I'm being nice she's simply *detail-oriented*.) I have close friends who were engaged for two years before they both had rings (she was waiting to find the perfect ring!) and some brides have an heirloom, while others buy both rings at once. The old tradition of the diamond ring proposal doesn't attract every hetero couple these days, so you can imagine lesbian couples have been doing their own thing for eons. Black diamonds? So popular with gay ladies. Alternative gemstones? Personalized jewelry? Even better. One bride-to-be I spoke to had a ring made out of tourmaline, a stone found in the Afghan mountain region where she and her fiancée had served in the Air Force.

What you'll hear from me most often throughout this book is that you and your bride are the key to this whole wedding thing. Remember, the wedding and all the events that surround it are the celebration of something much more meaningful—your marriage. Whenever possible, make it 100 percent about you as a couple. So if your idea of romance is getting matching tattoos around your ring fingers, do it. If you'd rather propose with the diamond studs your girl's been coveting for years, go for it. The reason I love hearing from women who submit their stories on 2brides2be.com is that they're all so confidently themselves. I love bold, stylish, unique couples who go full force in the direction of their shared dreams. That is love, and love is the bedrock of a marriage proposal.

Now, women are notoriously better when it comes to details. Yes, I realize this is an enormous generalization but I believe it. My proof? The proposal stories I have featured on my website. These brides have carved proposals into pumpkins, had custom-made cutlery and coffee mugs, they've planned scavenger hunts and flown in family, all to surprise their soon-to-be fiancées with the perfect proposal. Why did they go to such lengths? To ensure that the women they love had the proposal of her dreams. Carie loves breakfast in bed, so Kelley served up eggs, avocado toast, a side of grapefruit brulee, and a spoon etched with, "Will you marry me?" Oh, and of course this was all presented with Carie's favorite flower, peonies, and a vintage art-deco diamond ring. Lindsay loves brunch, so when she and Jackie hit up their favorite brunch spot, Jackie made sure that Lindsay's tea was served in a mug with a special message on the bottom, "Marry me, Linds." Tawnie planned a city-wide scavenger hunt, Jessica created a book and flew her girl to Paris, and Julie hired a secret photographer to capture her waterfront proposal.

My own wife, Sam, knows that a bonfire on the beach complete with s'mores and a bottle of wine are the surest way to get both my attention and my affection. Not only did she make these elements part of her proposal, but she used her storytelling skills to create a cartoon that told the story of how we met. When she finally convinced me to watch it, she secretly filmed the entire thing. (I did my part by wearing denim on denim and a loose ponytail—at least my manicure was on point.)

If you're thinking of proposing, then this is the question to ask yourself: what makes my girl smile?

Do you know she'll want her family close by? Or is she pretty low-key and private? Will she be touched if you propose in the restaurant where you had your first date? Or is she more of a lazy Sunday morning with tea and a side of diamonds?

### The proposal

The proposal is the cinder that sets the wedding flame. You'll be asked to tell the story countless times. You'll quickly be enveloped in a show of such love I can promise you'll be overwhelmed. This is the gunshot at the start of the race. This is the defining moment that sets the pace for all of the wedding jubilee that follows. Make it yours.

And if for some reason you don't know this yet, the question that immediately follows "show me the ring!" is this:

"So, when are you getting married?"

Unsolicited advice: if you're the woman planning on being asked, it's okay to give cues. Every single time I am complimented on my solitaire oval diamond ring, I first give props to my wife for spoiling me. Then I add, "Well, she knew what I wanted." It's okay to drop hints. It's okay to drag your girl into the jeweler in the mall and say, "Oh, I love a cushion cut." You're in New York City, walking down Fifth Avenue? Wander through Tiffany or Cartier and see what's new in high-end. Sure that a halo should never come anywhere near your hand? Let it be known! But don't be a curmudgeon. Don't nag. Women who wail and cry and throw tantrums do not deserve diamond rings or any other gemstones. They do not deserve thoughtful surprises and words of love.

Wanna know a secret? You're both women. If you simply cannot wait one minute longer to be engaged and you just know a tantrum is coming if your birthday passes and she doesn't propose—You do it. Go ahead. Problem solved.

But to be serious, it's important to be open and honest in your relationship about when you are ready for marriage. It's not just a wedding. This is a lifetime commitment you are making to each other, so make it count. Be kind to each other. Be thoughtful. And when necessary, be patient.

### *Hooray! You're engaged!*

Time to call your parents, text ring photos to your best friends, and overload all of your social media with your big news. This part gets overwhelming. It's craziness at full speed. If you got engaged in front of your entire extended family, then ignore this next bit, but if you got engaged privately at home or on vacation together then here's a tip: keep the engagement between the two of you.

I don't mean forever. I don't even mean for an entire day. But the second she slips that ring on your finger if you're Snapchatting and Instagramming then you're going to miss your own major milestone. Even if it's just one hour, enjoy that hour together. I had a built-in cushion. Sam proposed at night, in Oregon, so basically everyone we knew was already asleep. Eventually, after I polished off the bottle of wine we were drinking, I called my best friend who I assumed might still be awake. She was, and she was happy for me. Everyone else got the news the next day, which was still crazy overwhelming with the phone calls and texts but, *wow*, it was nice to have days of vacation left to enjoy our engagement just between us.

### So, now what?

What do you do first? Find a venue? Set a date? Call your favorite band?

For those of us planning a wedding who do not plan events for a living, this may be our only experience trying to put together an event of this magnitude. Naturally, it's overwhelming.

If you don't need to start planning immediately then don't. Being engaged is this blink in my life story, and it was so much fun. It was probably the most festive year of my life. Don't rush it.

When you are ready to talk planning, my advice is that you and your fiancée sit down, open a bottle of wine—or steep some tea—and talk about what your perfect wedding day looks like. Maybe you'll disagree completely, or maybe your ideas will link up exactly, but the hope is that you come through this conversation with a rough sketch of what matters most to you. Throughout this conversation you will both need to be patient and really listen to each other. It's okay to disagree, some things in life take a little time before we find the perfect compromise.

EXPERT TIP:

*Meg Nobile, Florist & Designer at That Time Events*

**What's the first thing you ask new clients?**

*How they met and what their spaces look like. We can go through months of design and we always end up with a beautiful reflection of the couple's space. If they are clean minimalists or vintage hoarders, we want to know.*

To get this conversation flowing you can both consider the following:

*What's your favorite way to celebrate?*

Do you like to get dressed up and go somewhere candlelit? Do you like all of your favorite people around you, or something more intimate? Maybe you prefer dancing to live music wearing your favorite jeans? Your party personalities can say a lot about the type of wedding you'd like to host.

*Where's a great place for your wedding?*

Considering who you're inviting, do you want your loved ones flying to the remote island where you took your first vacation? Do you think a January wedding in Mexico would be your dream come true? Do you love the place you call home? Or would you rather get married across the country, where you grew up?

*What do the two of you like to do together?*

Are you an outdoorsy couple who loves hiking and camping? Or are you more of a spa and fine-dining couple? Do you hate dancing but prefer long dinners with plenty of wine? Of course, many of us like camping and spas, long dinners and wild dance parties. It's not always easy to choose. I wish I could have had five weddings. All of them different. But the goal is one, so we must plan with this in mind.

*What do you hate most about weddings? What do you love most about weddings?*

We all do this. We attend a wedding and we can't help but whisper to each other, "Oh I love that, let's do it at ours," or, "Ugh, too many speeches." If there are traditions you'd rather skip—bouquet toss, anyone?—or elements you love, like an extended cocktail hour, then this is the time to tell each other.

## Who do you love to celebrate with?

Do you have a huge family and you're together for every occasion from Christmas to graduations to birthdays? Or do you have a smaller clan and a few intimate friends? Do you have weekly gab sessions at happy hour with twenty of your colleagues and can't imagine getting married without them? Now is the time to begin to take stock of the people who matter most to you both.

## Is religion a factor?

You may have religious or cultural customs that dictate much of your planning. Maybe it's a dream of yours to be married by your childhood pastor. Great, that might narrow down your location. Or maybe your hometown house of worship is the place. These factors can help spark the planning.

## How do you feel about moving around?

On my wedding day I did not want to have to deal with limos or trolleys or busses or any of it. Everything needed to be in one location. If you, however, have always dreamed of riding to your wedding in a white Rolls Royce, then you'll need a point A and a point B that have a road in between.

## EXPERT TIP

*Stephanie Karvellas-Baynton, Owner & Venue Coordinator at Cedar Lakes Estate*

**What's the most important detail brides should look for when choosing their venue?**

*A venue should do everything possible to make the event feel personalized for the couple. When your guests walk into your wedding you know you've succeeded when they say, "This is so them."*

Now you should have an idea, even if it's a very vague one, of what kind of wedding you and your fiancée are setting out to plan. Of course, budget is going to play an enormous role, that's just the cold, hard, truth, but don't worry about that yet. I promise you can have the wedding of your dreams within your budget. A bigger problem may be if your bride is dead-set on a destination wedding but you've always wanted to get married in the park by your childhood home. As you talk through these possibilities remember that it's not just about one of you. This day is yours as a couple, and you will find ways to compromise.

# What Comes First: the Venue or the Guest List?

**N**OW THAT NEWS OF your engagement is out, it's time to bring the focus back to you and your bride-to-be. You have some decisions to make early on. First, engagements excite people. You need to talk guest list pretty early in your planning process. Let me tell you why. For most of my wedding guests this was their "first ever" lesbian wedding. They were so excited. They wanted to tell everyone they knew about this big lesbian wedding. They couldn't wait to share pictures, two brides walking down the aisle. What would we be wearing? This was gonna be awesome… If this sounds at all familiar to you, it won't only be your family and friends who are excited at your engagement. Mere acquaintances will want to score an invite. Old friends you haven't really talked to in a while will congratulate you and ask you about your wedding plans. It's easy to get caught up in this excitement and tell everyone you know to save the date. Do not do this. You'll only have to backtrack once you emerge from your engagement fog and realize that you neither can nor want to invite that girl you haven't seen since eighth grade who occasionally likes your Facebook photos and wishes you a happy birthday every year.

Sam and I got engaged on vacation. We were on a beach in Oregon and drove to wine country the following day, where we proceeded to drink all of the pinot noir in Willamette Valley. We were excited and overwhelmed and we talked real fast and took pictures of our engagement rings and answered hundreds of texts and calls from our loved ones. After a couple of days there we drove to Portland, and over drafts of beer at McMenamins Kennedy School where I'd begged her to take me, Sam and I got into a heated whisper screaming match. We'd started out lovingly enough, talking hypothetical wedding plans and possible guest list numbers, and then we threw around names, and there came the disagreements.

You know that friend of your partner's that you can't stand? The one who always makes inappropriate lesbian jokes? Well, he may be sitting there when you're pronounced wife and wife. Our argument ended in a stalemate. Compromise comes easy to neither of us.

To avoid a screaming match with your new fiancée, I suggest you do the following. Sit down and make a hypothetical no-holds barred guest list. Add everyone you can dream of wanting at your wedding. Even if it's five hundred people long, go ahead and make this list. Neither one of you can nix a name. Make the big list and sit on it.

Days later, perhaps even a full week, look at the list again. Cross off the obvious names. Then take a red pen and star the names you do not agree on. Now, each bride-to-be can make her case for or against.

In the end what you must remember is that your wedding is not a celebration for one of you. Your wedding is about you as a couple, and if your future wife doesn't feel comfortable getting married in front of someone who has insulted her or with whom she really doesn't get along, it's important to respect that.

### What about inviting exes?

It's a cliché for a reason; many lesbians are friends with one or twenty of their exes. You'll hear mixed reactions as to whether exes should be invited to a wedding, but as with most things, I do believe there's a gray area. If you dated in your teens and have been friends ever since, I think it's safe to say you'd like them at your wedding. If you have a crazy ex-girlfriend who tried to make your fiancée's life a living hell early in your relationship, well, I think it wise that she not make the cut.

One of my favorite jokes during the course of wedding planning was that if I didn't let Sam invite exes, or friends she'd slept with in the past, then she wouldn't have anyone at the wedding. It's a bit of an exaggeration, but she and her friends were rather incestuous through high school. Something unique to every relationship, however, is jealousy. I have a lot of terrible qualities, but jealousy is generally not one of them (of course, there are exceptions to every rule). I didn't feel slighted or weird having these people as guests at our wedding. In reality, I'm actually friends with many of them now.

Use your judgment and don't be a jerk. You'll have to compromise, and try to do it without too many fighting words.

**Here's guest list advice I have given to countless friends**: *assume that this person you don't invite will never speak to you again. This is the worst-case scenario, right? Can you live with that? Your answer will let you know whether or not to invite them.*

If you're having a small wedding and really cannot accommodate many of the people you would like there, then that's understandable, too. Don't be afraid to talk to people. I had a friend who was terrified to mention her wedding. She thought that if someone asked her how the planning was going and she talked about it then she had to invite them. That's not the case. People are generally reasonable. As for the ones who aren't, see the worst-case scenario rule.

When it comes to people who are maybes, try to avoid telling them anything early on. You don't want to be the bride who mentions an invite then never sends it.

### Plus Ones?

This is one of the trickiest elements of the guest list debate. Everyone has an opinion on this. Single friends are notoriously pro plus one, and anyone who has ever planned a wedding is a little more fluid in their opinion on the matter.

*Are they traveling far? And alone? Do they know people at the wedding?*

For my own wedding, I implemented a hard rule about how long a couple had to be together. Unless it was a person traveling a long distance, I didn't want our single friends—of who we had many—bringing random Tinder dates to what would be one of the most memorable days of my life. Did some of them talk shit about this rule behind our backs? Maybe. Am I glad their exes are not in my photos? Hell yes.

**Once you start to get an idea of what you want your wedding to look like, your next big decisions will be your guest list and venue. Often, one helps determine the other**

*Guest list*

I was engaged for only a few days before Sam and I got into our first wedding argument—the guest list. Now is not necessarily the time to determine everyone you're going to invite, but now is the time to decide the ballpark on your guests. A budget of say, $25k, looks a lot different for 75 guests than it does for 250. Some brides have big families but also love their pals, others are only close with their parents and would rather celebrate with their best friends. Having an estimate of the number of guests you're inviting will help you determine your venue size, what you can splurge on and what you need to save on. A DJ, for instance, is the same price for any size crowd, but if you want that fourteen-dollars-per-slice cake, then you may not be able to feed dessert to a few hundred.

## The venue

Some couples already know they're going to get married at their family lake house, so the venue is locked in and they can choose a date around weather, or vendor availability. Some couples want their wedding in the restaurant where they had their first kiss over a plate of *linguine alle vongole*, and still other couples will have no idea where to get married. My wife and I had never discussed where to get married or agreed on a venue. We knew we wanted something outdoors, something out of the city, but from there we had to sit down and discuss. So we did.

The conversation went something like this:

Sam: I want great food that our guests will really enjoy.

Me: I want an awesome band, and no noise ordinances. If we wanna party all night then we're gonna party all night.

So just like that we'd narrowed down our venue search. We live in New York City and both love the wineries on Long Island's North Fork, but most of the venues out there have particular rules and their end times are firm. Don't get me wrong, that isn't to say they are not ideal places for many couples. But rules weren't going to work for us—goodbye vineyard wedding. We also weren't going to choose a wedding location that offered generic dining options or who weren't willing to work with us on designing our own menu.

Conversations like this help you make decisions without realizing it. Sam and I thought of a couple of wants, and just like that we got some answers about the wedding we wanted.

Armed with this small amount of information, we turned to the internet. We googled "rustic weddings New York." We leafed through back issues of bridal magazines and scanned their venue listings. We said, "Wouldn't it be great if we could rent a place and have our guests spend an entire weekend celebrating with us?"

Then Sam's aunt emailed her the name of an up and coming venue in Hudson Valley: Cedar Lakes Estate. They were only a couple years into hosting weddings—they didn't even have their own liquor license yet—but it was a family-owned place where we could have the all-inclusive weekend we were after. We called and scheduled a visit.

I told Sam: "Don't even bring the checkbook. We're just looking. We are not, under any circumstances, booking our wedding."

By the time we left that afternoon we had a wedding date and had paid a deposit. Of course Sam brought a check, and it took us only one tour of the grounds to know that this was our place. We got lucky. We also knew that if we visited too many venues we would never be able to choose, but that Cedar Lakes Estate could give us everything we were after.

So what happens if you look at many venues and still aren't sure? Once you know what kind of venue you want, then it's true that many of them are interchangeable. You want a barn wedding in Maine? A loft space in Brooklyn? Maybe a tented wedding in wine country? There are many venues to choose from, and this is when it comes down to details. Budget can also play a huge role in this choice. Can you spend half the price by moving your Brooklyn loft wedding to Queens? Then maybe you should do it. Is that barn in Maine going to be a little tight for 250 guests? These details will help you make bigger decisions.

If your dream is to marry on a Colorado mountaintop and celebrate in style at your favorite fine-dining eatery on the summit, then your guest list will inevitably be exclusive. If you've had your sights set on a ballroom in the Plaza Hotel since you were a little girl, then you're going to want more than a handful of loved ones to fill the space.

There's also the question of where you want your ceremony to be. Sure, these days many couples have their entire wedding in one location, but that doesn't mean you have to. If you want to say "I do" by the pond on your hometown village green, then consider a reception location close by. If you want your ceremony to be secluded and private, then you can plan a party anywhere, any time.

Also to think about—you are a same-sex couple, so naturally certain venues will not lend themselves to your wedding day, and that's okay. Plenty of two-bride weddings have taken place in houses of worship or been officiated by ministers. If you're looking for a religious ceremony followed by a celebration at another location, then make it happen. That's the beauty of your wedding—it's about the brides.

# Budget

FULL DISCLOSURE: MY WIFE and I blew our budget.

Why? We were not resolute.

Want to avoid this? You can. And you should.

Early in the planning process—before venues are booked and guest lists are complete—sit down together and make a budget. All of these moments when I advise you to sit down and do things together that are not really fun, these are all great times to open some of the champagne gifted to you on your engagement, lest you have bottles of Moët in your closet for years to come

First, create that holy-shit-weddings-are-expensive number. The number that represents your grand total, from dress to calligrapher to vendor gratuity. That number might feel ridiculous or imaginary, but whether this budget is $1,000, $10,000 or $100,000, write it down, and be realistic.

Next you'll break it down.

This is where your venue and wedding type will reveal itself in your budget planning. Are you getting married at a full-service venue with a price tag that includes everything? Or are you tenting the grounds at your aunt's mansion in Malibu? Now you know whether your budget includes rentals—tables, chairs, glassware, linens—or if this is all part of the package. Do you need to pay for lighting? Is your venue all-inclusive but you really want to spring for those pretty silver Chiavari chairs? Add this into your budget.

### Never forget: everything is extra

Next, talk to your family who may be helping foot the bill. Is your fiancée's mother springing for the rehearsal dinner? Have an uncle who wants to pay for the booze? Now's the time to gather this information, and it's important to have a specific amount. Of course, this can be awkward. And of course, the answer to how much your parents are willing to contribute might be zero dollars, but it's important to know early on. Maybe your parents are offering, but you and your fiancée agree that it's not worth it, that their money has too many strings attached. Now is the time to decide how much money the two of you can, and are willing to, spend.

My parents offered us a lump sum of money toward our wedding. I said to my mom, "I want you to pay for my dress, then we will use whatever money is left over toward our overall budget." My dress cost now came off the list and I didn't have to think about it any more. I'm a practical girl and I knew I wasn't going to blow a substantial amount of their money on a dress. Trust me, you can get your dream dress on a budget. Do not be fooled by high-end designers and their insane crazy price tags. We're not celebrities. Doesn't mean we don't get to look like one for a day.

If your wedding gown budget, for instance, is $2,500 then stick to it. How do you do this? You avoid boutiques that will push expensive dresses. You avoid boutiques whose price point starts at your max. You don't want to show up, excited to start trying on gowns, only to find that there are two dresses in stock in your range. Instead, find designers you like, and a retailer that carries a variety of silhouettes. If $2,500 is your budget then you want to go somewhere with dresses that start well below, and let your stylist know. They will be happy to accommodate. Don't forget that dresses might also require the following: tailoring, veil, shoes, accessories. Factor this in.

What to do: take that magic number and put it at the top of a blank sheet of paper. Now list every expense you can think of. List all of the vendors you will need for your venue and find out what these vendors cost in your area. A photographer in New York City, for instance, runs an average of $3,500 and above. The further in advance you book your wedding date, the more likely affordable vendors will still be available—so unless you need to plan a shotgun wedding, a longer timeframe means more money in your pocket.

Keep in mind—if your vendors need to travel, you're responsible for their travel and accommodation expenses.

## Budget Saving Tips

### Reduce your guest list

- No one wants to do this, but it's the easiest way to maintain your budget and still fulfill your wedding wish list.
- My advice? The excitement of an engagement can get the best of anybody, and suddenly we're texting ring pics with captions like, "Can't wait to celebrate with you" to pals we haven't spoken to since college. Enjoy your engagement. Get excited and talk nonstop about everything that's in store, but when it comes to potential guests you may need to cut from the list, it's best not to start with a promise of an invite.

### Find out if your venue offers any savings

- There are less popular times in the year that still make for beautiful weddings—snowy January nuptials anyone? These dates can mean the same wedding with huge savings.

- My advice? Okay, sure, you can save ten grand by getting married on a Thursday. That's simply not my style, and if you have guests who are traveling for the wedding they will seriously not appreciate a mid-week event. If, like me, you need that Saturday night autumn wedding, then don't beat yourself up. There are other ways to save.

### Plan ahead with stationary

- You'll need save-the-dates, wedding invitations, thank you cards, and postage. I forgot about a calligrapher until my invitations were already printed. Plan ahead so you can stick to your timeline and save some money. Rush orders never come cheap.
- My advice? If you're after custom letterpress invites, scale it down on your save-the-dates and thank-you cards. The invitations have the most impact on guests, so it makes sense to spend more on those.

### Find an affordable hair and makeup artist

- Most hair stylists or makeup artists have someone they love to work with. Let them team up or find a salon that can offer you both. Don't skip the trial. I know it seems like an added expense, but if your hair and makeup team know exactly what you're looking for on your wedding day, then you won't have to stress.

- My advice? No need to spend a fortune on wedding beauty, but you do want to love the way you look. Find a team who will use the price of your consultation toward your wedding day styling, and if you really love the way you do your own makeup, then get a tutorial instead and take care of your own face on your wedding day.

### Skip the plated meal

- Some weddings simply don't lend themselves to the seated, plated meal. Instead, find a dining option that works for you.
- My advice? If your guests will be on the dance floor all night and food will be an after thought, go for a reasonably priced buffet then spring for some passed desserts.

### Spend wisely on dessert

- If you're not into the idea of a giant wedding cake, then don't do it.
- My advice? Sure nobody's gonna eat that nine dollars-per-slice four-tier fondant cake? Create a dessert table and order a small cake for cutting.

### Don't blow your budget on the music

- If you don't absolutely need the ten-piece wedding band, then don't do it.
- My advice? Will your dance-floor vibe be more Top 40 than classics? Save on a DJ rather than

splurging on the band. Add an acoustic guitar and vocalist for your ceremony.

### Use seasonal flowers

- Trust your florist. You can spend a small fortune importing English roses, or insist on Dutch tulips in August, but, if you use what's in season, your florals will not only be more beautiful, they will be cheaper.
- My advice? Hire a local florist. That way he or she will know what's in season in your wedding location, and can steer you toward blossoms more in line with what you love.

### Cut back on the centerpieces

- Sure, gigantic centerpieces dripping with exotic orchids can be gorgeous in the right setting, but they're neither cheap nor practical.
- My advice? Supplement smaller centerpieces, or better yet alternate tables with candelabras and tea lights. Candles look stunning and blanket the room in a soft glow. Best of all, they're cheap. Have a theme going? Add stacks of vintage books, seashells, or wine bottles.

### Send a save-the-date postcard

- Sure, it's trendy, but trends exist for a reason. The cards will be cheaper and you'll also save on postage.
- Use an online stationer, search for a promo code, and order both your save-the-dates and your postage at once. Voila!

### Be stylish but smart

- Will your wedding be a disaster without Jimmy Choos on your feet? Splurge on your footwear but save on your accessories.
- My advice? Some bridal shops and designer showrooms charge hundreds for veils that you can easily have recreated for less money—even on Etsy. And did you know you can rent your accessories? If you're dreaming of five-carat diamond earrings with your updo, you can afford them for the day through sites like Adorn or Rent the Runway.

### Skip the limo

- I've never had a smooth experience with the limousines and shuttle busses for a wedding. They can't always be skipped, however, as sometimes both you and your guests need a ride to the venue.
- My advice? Plan ahead. If you choose a venue where you can have both the ceremony and reception, for instance—or better yet, a venue where you and your guests can stay—then there are no pesky transportation snafus. If you simply cannot avoid booking a limo or shuttle, cheapest is not always best. Find a company with great reviews and establish a relationship with an employee who knows exactly what it is you need on your wedding day.

### *Find an affordable planner*

- Many brides make the mistake of hiring a wedding planner when all they really need is a day-of coordinator.

- My advice? Meet with a few different coordinators to make sure they're on the same page with your vision of the day. Don't let them convince you to spend more than you need to. My wife and I were told that our wedding was too big for day-of coordination so we spent a small fortune on "partial planning," which was meant to include the initial and final three months of planning. This was wholly unnecessary, as we ended up taking care of most of the final details ourselves, with help from our wedding venue staff.

### *Skip the over-the-top after-party*

- Yes, they're a blast, but most guests are already drunk post-wedding, and they may not know the different between a dive-bar after-party that costs $500, or a fancy $5,000 soiree.

- My advice? Don't pay for bar staff. Organize a party where you can use the leftover reception booze, or guests can serve themselves. Sure, it's gonna get sloppy, but that's the fun of the after-party. And don't forget snacks. If it's possible, order a bunch of pizzas, turn on some music, and you've got a party.

### *Skip the menus*

- Why spend the extra money to list the food that everyone's likely expecting anyway? Haricort verts? Salmon with lemon dill beurre-blanc? Let the wait staff tell guests individually.

- My advice? If you're having food stations or a buffet then make larger signs that fit your aesthetic and include them on the serving tables.

### Skip the favors

- Unless the favor is edible, it usually gets lost or tossed.
- My advice? My wife and I skipped the favors altogether. We invested instead in an entire weekend of dining and entertainment for our guests. If your mother-in-law will simply die of embarrassment, make a donation to your favorite charity and print out a note for every place setting (or include on the menu, if you're having one) that says: "A donation has been made to the American Cancer Society in honor of our wedding guests."

### Skip the dancers

- Determined to hire a band and refuse to take no for an answer? I hear you. But are the five extra bodies on the floor—and extra spending for you—really necessary? Your guests can probably figure out the best way to get down to "Play That Funky Music."
- My advice? Don't spend extra on weird band or DJ shenanigans. Let's leave the boas and blow-up guitars in our memories of Bat Mitzvahs past.

### Budget your bar

- There's no reason to spring for top shelf for everyone. You and your bride want to sip on Grey Goose? Great. Let guests drink delicious-yet-lower-priced brands. If Uncle Pete cannot live without a single malt scotch, hide a bottle of Talisker behind the bar.

- My advice? Cash bars offend me. Avoid it at all costs. You can save money by providing an open bar at cocktail hour then switching to beer and wine for the reception. This allows guests to imbibe without costing you a fortune.

---

EXPERT TIP:

*Lisa Karvellas, Owner & Chef at Cedar Lakes Estate*

**What's your number one budget insider-savings tip?**

*Ditch the wedding cake! There are so many more affordable—and more delicious—dessert options.*

---

- And finally, allot about 5 percent of your budget for unforeseen expenses. Giving yourself a cushion means less stress.

# Your Wedding Binder

IN COLLEGE I HAD a summer internship in midtown Manhattan. It was my first—and one of my only—experiences working in corporate America. I worked on a top floor in an iconic high-rise. Women wore skirt-suits and I spent forty hours a week for ten weeks organizing invoices for their nonprofit subsidiary. I felt intimately connected to Elizabeth Hurley, the face of their campaign, and I kept haphazard piles of documents on my desk. When my superior wrote me a glowing review at the end of my time with her, she also included the only weakness she could see in my daily routine. She wrote something like: *while it never adversely impacts her work, Laura's desk is slightly disorganized.*

That's me. My messes aren't messy to me, but my organization is in no way pristine.

My wife color codes her closet and alphabetizes her DVD collection. When she calls me messy I take offense—she's just abnormally obsessive. She makes detailed binders every time we travel. There are tabs: Hospitals, Hotels, Maps, Restaurants.

Naturally she had rules for our wedding binder. She didn't want me shoving magazine articles or invoices in there haphazardly. She wanted everything labeled and organized.

## *Organization Tips*

- Make a wedding website. If you're not techy or don't feel like spending money on a domain name, don't worry about it. You can go through any of the major wedding websites and most will let you host a basic site for free. This site will simplify your lives when friends and family are asking a million questions about accommodations and dress codes. You can share your proposal story on the site, bios of your wedding party, registry information, even your honeymoon location with the option for guests to donate money rather than sending you a blender. Send the URL out into your social media and email it to Mom, who can send it along to the rest of the family.

- Make a wedding-only email. This is easy. Add an account to your Gmail or Hotmail or Yahoo or whatever it is you use and keep all of your wedding emails separate form your personal accounts. Add folders to the wedding inbox: photographer, caterer, florist, etc. You won't regret this. The email address can be anything. It can be your names, your wedding hash tag, whatever: "AmyandJenWedding" or "MichaelsonWedding" or "MrsandMrsC2B" at gmail, yahoo, or hotmail. You get it. (The only correspondence I kept in my personal account were my dress emails, for obvious reasons.)

- The first page in your wedding binder should be contact information for all of your vendors. Then create sections and file your contracts into its place. You do not want to lose signed contracts, receipts, or proofs of deposits. Keeping them in your binder means you'll always know where to find them.

- Next should be your budget: write down your wants. (I try to avoid saying "must-haves" because if you cannot have it, well, the show must go on.) Did your friend have a rock star videographer at his wedding? Get the information. Will mascara tears run down your face if your favorite artist doesn't do your wedding makeup? Make a list of these desires so you tackle them first.

- Keep a calendar in your binder. Every wedding publication and every book has one of those monthly checklists of all the things you should have done by now. These are merely suggestions and if they're just going to up your stress factor, ignore them. But if your wedding is in two months and you don't have an officiant, well, you will need to get on top of it. These checklists are a good guideline for some of the big decisions you have to make early in the planning process. What I find to be better than those generic checklists are personalized ones, and the best way to do that, once you've hired all of your vendors, is to call them. Call the shuttle company and ask them when you need to confirm your times. Mark your calendar for that date, as well as one month ahead of time. **Extra check-ins never hurt**. Let them call you a nag or a bridezilla, but you're allowed to be firm on this communication. Ask your officiant your deadlines for ceremony readings, rituals, and vows. Mark your calendar. Still haven't decided what to wear? Most suit makers and dressmakers need at least a few months for measurements, so mark your calendar. Once you've taken the time to create these deadlines for yourself, your monthly checklist creates itself.

*Example*

We chose our wedding venue in fall. We chose our wedding date for the following fall. Suddenly we had a twelve-month countdown. So we prioritized. I researched photographers and made consultation appointments. I emailed the band I'd had my eye on for years, and we began to do research on officiants. Bummer, the band was already booked. They suggested another band, so Sam and I made plans to see them play while I booked a meeting with a music agent. I wanted options. These vendors created their own timeline: the officiant gave us homework and a deadline to send her our story and loved ones with whom she could chat about us. She gave us another deadline to choose ceremony readings. The music agent played me a band that sounded great, so while he held our wedding date we made plans to see them play live. Our venue told us we would need to purchase event insurance six months out. Added that to the calendar. Dress shopping would be fun, I thought, but I didn't need to schedule appointments until winter. The florist and event designer, meanwhile, needed to start planning how to fit nearly 175 guests into a ceremony space designed to seat half that. Our venue was in a small town, so I found the nearest hotels and booked room blocks. I had no guesses on hair and makeup, so I began reaching out to people who might. I knew I had time. Okay, we thought, big decisions have been settled. Let's plan an engagement party and meet with a stationer.

- If you're an avid Pinterest user keep your images organized. Whether you find photos on wedding blogs or other sites, print out photos you want to show to your designer and keep them in your binder.
- Make a list! Before the final guest list make a TO DO list, including all vendors and extras you have to handle. For example: we had to organize how many guests could stay on the property and who to put in which cabins. We had to book hotel blocks in local hotels. Those guests needed to be shuttled to the wedding. We had to rent golf carts and get insurance to use them at our venue. We had to rent our own linens. We had to purchase our own liquor (more on that later—stress is trying to stock a bar for 175 drinkers). This list goes on. If your venue is very much a blank space, then you have a lot on your plate—

and that's okay. The best, most unique weddings sometimes take a lot of careful planning.

Knowing everything you have to do is slightly horrifying when you take a look at all of it, but once you have a list you can prioritize, so don't be afraid to get going on it. And if you're hiring a wedding planner, do this early. He or she will be able to help you meet deadlines and keep your priorities straight. If you're not delegating some of the big tasks to them then you're wasting your money.

EXPERT TIP:

*Sharon Becker, Makeup Artist*

**How can a bride put her own twist on a classic element?**

*Play with color and shape. Incorporate a color on the eye or lip that is not found in the boring bridal mags, and make it your own. For an updo try a textured "faux-hawk" that will get your hair off your face, make you look modern, but still incorporate the updo elements that look so great on camera.*

# Engagement Party or Not?

**W**ANT TO KICK OFF the celebration with an engagement party? Great! Have no idea who to invite or when to have it or where to have it? No problem. That will come.

First, of course, is always budget. Do you want a blow-out? Or does brunch with mimosas and your best friends sound perfect? Maybe your parents want to host a family BBQ in their backyard, or your dad wants to invite your friends to his country club. If someone is offering to throw you a party, unless there are deal-breaking strings attached, you should accept. Maybe a backyard BBQ wasn't the cocktail-party-on-the-water you've always dreamed of. So what? Wear whatever you like, sip whatever you like, and enjoy the first of many celebrations where you and your beloved are the guests of honor. It's overwhelming to be the center of attention in this way. It can be especially intense as a lesbian couple. For many of us this is our first time with our families, all eyes on us, as we all openly celebrate this relationship. *Gulp*. My advice is that an engagement party, no matter how big or small, gets everyone's engines revving for the lesbian wedding.

Throwing my big Catholic family with Sam's big Jewish family and adding all of our wild friends was a daunting but exciting prospect. "Let's rip the band-aid off!" we decided. "Let's get crazy!"

As is typical of parents, mine determined the date of my engagement party—not because they were paying for it, but because they were traveling. A lot. They preferred something in late December. Okay, so the outdoor venues were out. Because we wouldn't be getting married in our home city of New York, we knew we wanted our engagement party here. Once we got past the frustration of trying to find an affordable venue around the holidays, we really warmed up to the idea of a holiday engagement party. I'd fallen in love with a gold sequined dress that summer, and now I had a reason to wear it. Sam and I imagined candlelight and strong cocktails, cupcakes and tall Christmas trees. We got pretty excited for an intimate holiday engagement soirée.

We found an amazing venue in Brooklyn—a bar called Larry Lawrence—and knew that its exposed brick and wood paneling would give us the intimate vibe we were after. They didn't have their own kitchen but recommended a local restaurant who could cater. We went for dinner one night and loved it. An order of Sprinkles cupcakes and we were all set.

We didn't want to inconvenience anyone too much—we were already asking everyone to go to Brooklyn—so we let faraway friends know about the party in case they happened to be in town, but we had no expectations of anyone making the trip. "Save your airfare for the wedding," we told them. We requested *No Gifts* on our invitations, but added donation information in memory of Sam's mom. That way anyone who could not resist giving could help a good cause.

The rest was very much our idea of a good time. I've been to many engagement parties, and they're always a fantastic occasion if the newly engaged couple is having a good time with their loved ones who are excited to celebrate them through the months ahead. You don't have to have your wedding planned or all the details figured out to have an engagement party. If you really don't know what your guest list is going to look like then simply invite family and your closest friends. Avoid inviting anyone you're certain won't be invited to your wedding—unless you're planning to elope, then you have some wiggle room.

What goes down at an engagement party can be totally up to you. Often there are speeches and introductions. Sometimes there's an embarrassing slideshow of the couple as toddlers, or maybe it's just a time to sip cocktails with your favorite people.

Sam had not only made a cartoon for her wedding proposal, but she secretly recorded me watching it then edited the video. Friends and family were asking to see it, so early in the night we spoke some warm words to our guests then showed them all the video. (Maybe not everyone wanted to see it, but so what, it was five minutes long.) I think this was a special moment to share with loved ones who had never seen us as a couple in a romantic or unguarded setting, and I really enjoyed kicking off our engagement this way. After that it was all about boozing, dancing, and having a blast. Oh, and here's advice for anyone who likes to let loose: take some nice photos early in the night. This way you have gorgeous photos and you won't wake up the next morning kicking yourself for forgetting to take that adorable photo in front of the Christmas tree.

Sam's parents were married at the Plaza Hotel in New York City in December 1981. Swanky, right? Sam and her brother had spent their childhoods perusing the wedding albums and even I'd seen more than a few photos of their big day. Her mom loved calla lilies and used them as centerpieces at her own wedding, so for our December engagement party Sam brought a photo to our local florist and had them recreate the centerpieces. We only had a few made, to line the bar, but they were a special nod to her parents, especially her mom.

EXPERT TIP:

*Meg Nobile, Florist & Designer, That Time Events*

**What's the biggest mistake you see brides making?**

*Not enjoying the process. I know things can be stressful but the whole ride matters too. That's why it's so important to hire people you feel comfortable with and confident in.*

*Engagement party pointers*

- If you know you're having a 250-plus black tie wedding, have a clam bake or backyard BBQ to kick off your wedding festivities on a laid-back note.

- If your wedding plans are still a mystery to you and your new fiancée, go ahead and plan a gathering that works for the season and your budget.

- If you're already registered that's fine, many guests will know to shop off that list, but don't add it into the invitation. This can be seen as tacky. If you're planning not just this engagement party but also a shower and the wedding, you may want to let guests know that gifts are not necessary. This can be added to the invitation. This allows the party to be a kick-off for the celebrations ahead, but also a gift to your loved ones that says, "We know you're going to do a lot for us in the months ahead, this is our way of saying thanks."

- Wanna wear white? Wear white! You're brides now.
- Make a speech. Again, this is the first of what might be many events ahead. Say a few words.
- Introduce everyone. Not only should your families be intermingling by now, but your friends, too. This way when the wedding rolls around many of your guests will feel like old friends.
- You can totally send electronic invitations and save yourself the money and effort of stationary and postage, but you will need to mail real thank you cards.

If an engagement party isn't your thing, that's cool, too. You will have plenty of opportunities ahead to celebrate with loved ones.

# PART TWO

## The Couple

**P**LANNING A TWO-BRIDE WEDDING has all the trimmings of an *alternative* or *nontraditional* wedding, but that's not necessarily the case. Some lesbian couples want the church ceremony, the white dress, first dance, cake-cutting—all the elements we've come to think of when we talk about "traditional weddings." And some lesbian couples want to scrap some or all of those elements. White dresses and bouquet tosses? Not for all of us. Our sexuality does not define our every desire, but who we are marrying certainly affects what kind of wedding we want.

A wedding is not just a party, and it is never about one person. It's about you as a couple, and the people who love you. If you let this truth rule from the moment you say "yes" to the moment you say "I do," then the rest is cake.

# What Kind of Couple are You?

**M**Y WIFE AND I do not have some unique hobby that like, totally defines us. I enjoy hiking, and a few times a year I manage to drag her out into the woods. We love pumpkin picking in fall and hitting the beach in summer. We don't have a local bar where we're weekend regulars. We don't have a table at some little Italian joint where we order the same dish every Friday. We love our dogs, okay, but we weren't going to plan a wedding around that. Does this sound familiar? If not, and you're both avid rock climbers who are going to weave this passion into your wedding plans, then good on you. For the rest of us, we have to rediscover some of the details that make us, well, us.

There are easy ways to incorporate your couple characteristics into your wedding, like your proposal. I was making s'mores by a bonfire when Sam popped the question. Our wedding venue had an open-air fire pit in their dining pavilion and had house-made marshmallows. No brainer. Other details you have to smoke out a little. Here's some help:

- **Where did you meet?** Did you spot her across the room at happy hour? Maybe you met on your college campus or perhaps you let technology help and found each other online. Whatever the answer, you can pay homage, whether it's with your stationary—movie ticket invites that represent your first date—or table numbers categorized by drink names at your favorite college bar. AmberBock anyone?

- **What's your favorite food?** Does your fiancée make a mean grilled cheese? Do you order Thai food every other night? Incorporate these favorites into your menu. Maybe you'll have passed grilled cheese sliders at cocktail hour, or the dumplings from your favorite Thai restaurant for guests to munch on at the after-party.

- **What do you drink?** Do you love making sangria at home on Saturday afternoons? Make this your signature cocktail. Sam loves tequila. I do not. I love whipped cream vodka. Sam does not. (Neither do any of my friends, apparently.) We had passed shots of both spirits during dessert at our wedding reception. Was this a good idea? That's still up for debate.

- **What's your favorite flower?** Sam loves sunflowers. I didn't want them featured during our wedding ceremony or reception, so they became the centerpiece for our bridal shower, as well as incorporated into floral design throughout our wedding weekend.

- **What's your favorite book?** Have you read *Mrs. Dalloway* ten times? Did your fiancée buy you a book of romantic poems for your first Valentine's Day as a couple? What about using one of these for a reading during your ceremony? Same goes for lines from favorite movies or songs.

- **What's your favorite music?** Do you like Top 40? Or does classic rock get you both on the dance floor? How about Motown? Speaking of songs, maybe your band or DJ can tackle an instrumental version of that song you danced to at a dive bar the first time you met. Music has more uses than the obvious ceremony and reception uses. Song lyrics go great in speeches and readings, you can even plan an entire shower around the theme "all you need is love." Or, if you're more of a couple who likes to be tongue in cheek, use the theme "come to my window."

- **Do you vacation in the same place every year?** Some couples choose to get married in their favorite travel destination. Others incorporate an element into their wedding. Love New Orleans? You don't have to be down south to have a second line after your ceremony. Spend one week every summer on Nantucket? A tented clambake makes for a great rehearsal dinner or reception idea.

- **Do one or both of you excel at something?** Is your fiancée a great bowler but you like to hang around and drink beer? Go bowling after your rehearsal dinner, or host your bridal shower at a bowling alley. You'll feel like a kid again and none of your guests will forget your unique take on traditional wedding rituals.

- **What are your ethnic backgrounds?** There are the obvious: hello jumping the broom or dancing the hora. Then there are other details you can explore: a Celtic hand fasting during our ceremony was a nod to my Irish roots. Brides Dinah and Malila had a caterer infuse their wedding food with culture, serving both Latino food and soul food to represent both brides' backgrounds.

This is only a start. I'm sure the wheels are turning now.

## EXPERT TIP:

*Elizabeth Phaire, Master Life-Cycle Celebrant® and Interfaith Minister*

### What's your most frequent request?

*For a ceremony that is "spiritual but not religious." Many couples believe in a universal higher power and/or connect deeply with nature, but don't follow a specific religious path or deity. They want a spiritual ceremony that has depth, speaks to their love, the bonds of family, and what marriage means for them.*

# Know Your Rights

O N JUNE 26, 2015, the US Supreme Court ruled that gay marriage is a right protected by the US Constitution in all fifty states. Prior to their decision, same-sex marriage was already legal in thirty-seven states and Washington, DC, but was banned in the remaining thirteen.[2]

It seems as if today in the United States the rights of same-sex couples are ever-changing. Just as we (finally) win our right to marry, we're faced with backlash and discrimination from both private and public sectors. Sadly, planning a same-sex wedding can expose you and your bride-to-be to the possibility of discrimination. This can be determined by where you live and what kind of wedding you're planning, and we'll talk more about familial support ahead, but it's also important that you have the encouragement of both your community and your vendors.

I planned a wedding in New York State and most of my vendors were based in New York City, which meant that for many of them, this was not their first same-sex wedding. Though we raised a few eyebrows and I had to answer many questions with, "There is no groom, the other bride's name is Samantha," we were met with nothing but joy and even excitement that felt genuine. We know, still,

Information from Procon.org

how fortunate we are, and that many couples face just the opposite.

### *Here are some tips to ensure that you too get the treatment that you deserve*

Your venue is the beating heart of your wedding, with your vendors serving as veins and valves and other metaphorical body parts. Select a venue where you feel comfortable, accepted, and celebrated. This is good advice for all couples. Unless you're getting married in a private residence then yes, we all know that other couples have come before and will come after us at our chosen venues, but during the planning process right through to the minute you drive away post-wedding, you want to feel like the beloved leaders of a fairy tale kingdom.

I've read too many stories of the discriminatory baker who wouldn't bake the "gay wedding cake," and I've watched as these stories propelled unassuming same-sex couples and business owners into the public eye. These situations don't look to end well for anyone, but I can say with certainty that every single time, the couple is humiliated. This is not a feeling we want, recall when we think back on our wedding.

My rule of thumb is ridiculously simple. When seeking out photographers, for instance, I click onto their website and explore their portfolio. Nine times out of ten an LGBT-friendly photographer will have a same-sex couple featured on their site. Of course, this isn't always the case. I collaborate with creatives often who insist they'd love to shoot a lesbian wedding, but they simply haven't been asked yet. We can also spin these discriminatory-cake-baker stories and use our "otherness" to our advantage. We had one vendor willing to drop her prices significantly because she wanted us in her portfolio. I reminded my wife of this often, "Babe, we are two women. I'm wearing a custom green wedding gown, you're wearing Vera Wang, we're throwing this big expensive weekend in the woods. We are a prize, so let's behave accordingly." Of course, it's easy to say this to her, then get super shy when actually interacting with vendors.

If you're booking vendors blindly you need only reach out with basic information.

> *Hello. We are Jennifer and Marissa and we're thrilled to tell you that we are planning a lakefront wedding next August and are looking for a photographer with a great editorial eye.*

When choosing our wedding photographer— Heather Waraksa—this was my initial email:

> *My fiancée Samantha and I are planning a wedding weekend extravaganza at the beautiful Cedar Lakes Estate next September. We are trying to get on top of some of the*

*planning. As two girls, we both have some strong opinions on this wedding, but so far we're (surprisingly) seeing incredibly eye-to-eye. My one major concern is photography! I don't really like the look of most wedding photos, and I'd like something a bit different, specifically someone who can snap those magic moments and make it look effortless.*

*We think your portfolio is incredible and would love to learn more about you and let you learn more about us.*

*Our weekend will include a lakeside BBQ, mountaintop toasts, swimming and sports, vows by the lake, a big reception in a gorgeous barn, and an after-party in the "tree house." We think it's going to be spectacular and we're looking for the right person to help capture the celebration.*

*If you think you may be interested, and of course, available, we would love to meet you.*

This is essentially the email we sent to every single vendor, with a few tweaks of course. We also created a wedding-only email address: 2Brides2Be. Our excitement was infectious and we had amazing vendors onboard pretty quickly. As is reflective of my personality, I wanted to give plenty of information up front. I wanted potential vendors to know what kind of couple we were and what kind of wedding this was going to be.

My advice is to be up front about you as a couple, the wedding you want, and the kind of people you want to work with to make it a reality. There are going to be awkward moments—one dress consultant asked if mine was a "double wedding" when I told her there would be two brides—but I've never met a single person in a same-sex couple who isn't used to the occasional awkward moments. I have no problem with those. In fact, I like being able to help others feel comfortable with how to speak to us and become more inclusive in their business practices. Be open. If you're sick of crossing out the word "Groom" then suggest to your vendors, "Maybe you should create documents with alternate wording."

> *It's not that tough to change their forms to read:*
>
> *Spouse #1 _____*
>
> *Spouse #2 _____*
>
> *Let's not be afraid to ask.*

*Tips:*

- Know your rights, really. There are still places in the USA where it's legal to discriminate against people who are LGBT-identified. Sure, if the bakery you're interested in turns out to be an establishment of bigotry and you don't feel like dealing with it, you can find another bakery. But if there's a Kim Davis on the loose who will try to hinder your legal right to marriage, contact a local LGBT resource for help. (And if you want to take that bigoted baker to task, I support you!)

- Do early research. Brides Betsy and Jenna both grew up Catholic and wanted to incorporate their faith into their wedding ceremony. They found a local Catholic church that is accepting of everyone, and when they met with the priest they knew he was perfect for them.

- If a vendor gives you a bad vibe, don't hire them. I'm an avid supporter of avoiding people who make you uncomfortable for any reason. Even if you can't quite put your finger on it, your feelings are valid.

- Maintain a sense of humor. You might be stuck crossing out the word "Groom" a few times or find yourself repeating, "No, my fiancée is female." Don't get frustrated or vicious. People are used to their own habits and they're comfortable with what they know. Often no one is trying to insult you and they'll be glad for the education if you're polite and open.

- Lend an ear. Many of your vendors will have a lesbian friend or sister they want to tell you about. Of course this is normal in the gay community, so you might be used to it. They're trying to connect with you, it's a good sign.

- Don't let anyone get away with offending you. Again, sometimes people don't even know they're committing a faux pas. Don't be afraid to say, "Actually, we prefer to be referred to as this," or, "No neither one of us is 'the groom.' This is an offensive misconception." It's not our job to be the teacher, but I try to remind myself, *if not me, who?*

## EXPERT TIP:

*Daniel Friedman, Bindle & Keep bespoke suitmaker*

### What's your number one insider budget-saving tip?

*Do what I do, go kids clothes whenever possible. For those who can fit into the upper bodies of boys clothing, you'll save a ton a money without losing out on quality. I've seen too many clients spend north of $150 on adult bowties that are unfashionably large and only serve to overwhelm their faces. I wear boys accessories all the time because they jive with my proportions better and thankfully cost a tenth the price.*

# Coming Out

SURE, TO SOME IT may sound strange. They may throw up their hands, palms to the sky and say, "How can you be planning a wedding if you haven't even come out yet?"

To this I say two things. First, some of us do things differently, outside the sphere of whatever is considered the *normal* path, and we're cool with that. Second, this happens all the time. So if you find yourself engaged and reading this book and you haven't *come out* yet, I promise you this: you are not alone.

Okay so first, what do I mean by coming out? I myself am turned off by the phrase. I think of Robin Williams and Nathan Lane in *The Birdcage*. (If you haven't seen this film, you must, but I warn you, watching this will make you miss Robin Williams more than ever.) There's something so Miami-gay-in-the-eighties that *coming out* evokes for me. (I was born in 1985 but that's neither here nor there.) When I use the phrase "coming out" I mean any and all of the ways in which you got from point A to point B.

Point A) I'm in love with a girl *or* I have a crush on a girl *or* I think I like girls.

Point B) I'm getting married and my family knows and my friends know and my coworkers know and my fiancée is a babe and our wedding is going to be awesome.

I understand that lesbian wedding guest lists run the gamut of "everyone we have ever loved is here to support us—hooray!" to "we invited only the friends and family who are supportive of our right to marry" to "we don't really talk to our families so we're eloping." Same-sex weddings cover these options and all of those in between. (More on this in the upcoming chapter—"Family.") Sure, there are hetero couples who face disapproval, some who don't get along with their families, I'm not excluding them, but to write a wedding guide that features advice and practical planning for two women getting married, I would be remiss not to acknowledge that LGBTQ-identified couples don't always have it easy.

That being said, here's the part where I remind you that there are no rules and that my advice always comes with addendums. I do, however, say this with conviction: *you will regret it if you do not come out to your loved ones.*

Maybe you're secretly engaged and you're just starting to share the news with your family. Maybe you're dating a woman for the first time and as you fall more and more in love with her you realize, "Okay, this is real, maybe I should stop hiding this." Hello, you're in love. This is amazing. Frolic in meadows. Kiss in the rain. Daydream at the traffic light until everyone's beeping at you.

I realize why many younger couples might have an easier time including family and friends in their nuptials. Sam and I have been a part of each other's families since college. By the time wedding planning was a part of our lives, everyone from old high school buddies with whom we'd lost touch to second cousins to grandparents knew we were a couple. We were able to lay the groundwork over many years, and for that I know we are fortunate. I understand too that there are couples who have been together secretly for years. Family and friends know them as "best friends," and the burden of coming out involves a degree of shame for hiding this secret. Says one newly engaged bride-to-be, "I lied to them for so long. I don't want them to hate me."

If this sounds familiar then don't worry. Take a deep breath and decide, as a couple, how to handle the coming out process. Maybe you're planning a wedding that is say, six months away, and you want to invite your whole family but every time there's an opportunity to tell them you chicken out. Understandable. This is scary. You've thought of all of their terrifying reactions, all of their mortifying questions and how they'll undoubtedly look at your differently. It's true. Some people are going to look at you differently. So what? Your loved ones are the people that matter. There will be plenty of times when you are ogled by complete strangers, so don't be afraid of a few raised eyebrows from your aunts and uncles.

Here's something else to keep in mind. If that wedding date is approaching and you still haven't come out to half your guest list, think about other weddings you've attended. The best ones are not the ones in which your second cousin is marrying some guy you met once at Grandpa's funeral. The best weddings are the ones in which you know the couple as just that, a couple. The more time you give your loved ones to see you together, interacting not as "roommates" or "coworkers" but as a full-blown lesbian couple, the less shocked they'll be watching you lock lips on your big day. My family knew Sam and I as a couple for years before we got engaged, but part of our engagement party was introducing our extended family to the romance aspect of our relationship. We'd kept this pretty much to ourselves, and wedding planning let us ease everyone into the idea that yes, we are best friends and partners, but that we are also in love with each other.

There are also couples whom, for all intents and purposes, are "out," but prefer to leave their personal lives away from the office. Sound familiar? Maybe you're surrounded by love and support from family and friends but feel, and rightfully so, a degree of apprehension about opening up to coworkers. But let's see, what do all brides in the throes of wedding planning have in common? It's almost all they talk about.

When I was twenty-three and living with Sam in LA I got a job at a cable ad sales company. My coworkers were awesome but all the other assistants talked about were their boyfriends and fiancées. I didn't know these girls very well and I was new to LA, which meant I had only a few friends. I was so nervous to come out at work. After a few months there my boss took the assistants out to lunch. One of the girls looked at the claddagh ring on my finger and said, "Doesn't that mean you're in love?" I wasn't going to blatantly lie so I told her that yes, I was in love, that I actually moved to LA with my girlfriend. The moment was awkward for sure. I am positive that my whole body was blushing, but the moment I said it I felt more comfortable. The coworkers who were accepting and interested in hearing about my life and seeing pictures of Sam made themselves apparent, and anyone who wasn't into it, well, they didn't have to eat lunch with me. Sam, meanwhile, was working at a big-name Hollywood agency. Not only did her boss know nothing about her, she didn't want to. This was not an environment where assistants shared personal details. Sam finally confided in a coworker, mostly because she was sure that one girl on her floor was also a lesbian. This made work-life much easier for Sam, and eventually I got to meet many of her coworkers and wow them with my good looks and great conversational skills.

I know there are also couples living in parts of the country or working in fields where coming out might jeopardize their careers. This bigotry breaks my heart, but sadly, it's still a reality for many couples. I know a couple who are in this situation, and they still pulled off a gorgeous wedding with all of their loved ones in attendance. Those who matter will show up for you.

This rant has a point. Maybe you and your bride-to-be began a life together over a decade ago. Maybe you already have children. Maybe you're divorced from a man and had no idea you could fall in love with a woman. Maybe you both want kids and when you met you just knew that there was no reason to wait and you're planning a wedding while still fitting your lives together. Whatever is going on in your relationship, wedding planning should be full of joy. I really, really mean this, so I am going to say it again. Planning your wedding should be one of the highlights of your entire relationship. Of course there will be stressful moments, but the time leading up to the day you become wife and wife should full of love. You should be surrounded by the people who love you both, the ones you're grateful for in your life. Let them in. If not all of them, then you know which ones. They want to be there to lend a hand, or take you dress shopping, or plan a bachelorette party. They want to give a toast in your honor and tell embarrassing stories from high school. They want to see you happy, and if there are people in your life who would rather see you alone than with a woman, then screw 'em. You found the love of your life, you're going to get married. So come out, come out wherever you are!

### Tips on Coming Out:

- As I've gotten older I've learned the value of a face-to-face conversation. Sure, sometimes a letter is the only way. Sometimes an email feels easier, but if you can get in the same room with whomever you want to speak to, then you should.
- It gets easier. The more people you tell, the easier it becomes, but that's not to say this isn't a grueling task. Still, anyone you love and respect should hear it from you, not a messenger.
- Bring back-up. You don't have to do this alone. Have your fiancée and siblings present if you're certain your mom is going to freak out.
- Don't get defensive. There's no need to start the conversation with a combative tone. Be zen.
- Try to be open to the inevitable questions.
- Don't apologize.
- Once you've told your loved ones, social media is a real easy way to spread the message to the masses, if you're into that kind of thing.

EXPERT TIP:

*Chelsea Mason, Photographer*

**What's your most frequent request?**

*The request that I most frequently receive is getting asked if I'm okay with breaking tradition. My answer: OF COURSE! It is YOUR big day, not mine! Let's put a twist on your day to make your images stand out from the rest.*

# *Family*

RELATIONSHIPS ARE HARD ENOUGH without the added anxiety of worrying about what our families might think.

Weddings, of course, are all about love. And what makes family, if not love? Sadly, some LGBT-identified couples face discrimination from their own family, which can add an emotional toll to wedding planning. An already high-stress time in many couples' relationship, wedding planning is usually made easier by the excitement and support of loved ones. But what happens when that's not the case? Some brides-to-be face a wedding without some or all of their family. Others make peace with having an aunt in attendance who doesn't believe in their right to marry but wants to attend anyway. While each individual must deal with their own circumstances differently, it's important to know that, if you're facing discrimination, you are not alone.

I was fortunate in my wedding planning, because if I had any family in attendance who did not agree with my right to marry they did not say so. I felt tremendous love and support throughout every single event—my engagement party, bridal shower, and the entire planning process. It was not lost on me, however, how lucky I am. I've heard from many women since I took my relationship public and most often the fear confessed to me is that they will lose the love of their family.

I think it's worth noting, first and foremost, that often the fear is worse than the reality. I know my own mom needed time to get used to the idea that I was dating a woman. This did not happen overnight, and I did something that does not come easy to me—I was patient. I want to live in a world where a woman doesn't have to come out, when a same-sex relationship isn't under constant scrutiny, when we aren't faced with bigotry. Until then, it's important that we give our loved ones both time and the benefit of the doubt.

My mom likes to tell the story of how she shared the news of my upcoming marriage with her father, my Grandpa Keller. Grandpa already knew "my friend" Sam, and we suspected that he knew the real nature of our relationship, but as tends to happen with grandparents, we kept our mouths shut for his benefit. Or what we thought was his benefit. I'm learning that leaving your loved ones out of your life never actually benefits anyone.

Mom said to him, "Daddy, I have good news and I have bad news. The good news is Laura Leigh is getting married. The bad news is that she's marrying Sam."

Let me just say that I have no idea why she spoke this way. She and the rest of my family had been supportive of my relationship for many years.

I think her words were meant to make Grandpa feel comfortable with any reaction. And he did react. He said, "I've been wondering when you were gonna tell me."

That was it. From that day forward he asked about wedding plans during our weekly chats, and counted down the days until the big weekend. Grandpa had a blast at our wedding. He laughed with my friends and danced with me and my new wife. He was the first to call us on our one-year anniversary and wish us love and happiness, and Sam and I spent his final months visiting him both at home and in hospice. He was so proud and loving to not only me, his granddaughter, but to my wife as well.

I know. The conversation doesn't always go this way. For Lauren, who is not yet married, revealing her relationship to her family was an obstacle that took a lot of courage.

Before she could introduce her girlfriend Jess to her family in Arkansas, Lauren needed to tell them about her. She wrote her grandparents a letter.

(Opening up to family about a personal relationship is emotionally exhausting. There is over-thinking and paranoia and the burden of feeling like your relationship is under the microscope.)

Lauren was kind enough to let me read her Granddad's email that he sent her in reply. He stated explicitly that both he and Lauren's grandmother are Christians who believe that marriage is between a man and a woman, that they "truly believe in an 'Adam and Eve' whom God ordained and began our civilization as we know it." Lauren admitted to me that she thought of various ways to respond to his email, which ended with this poignant declaration: "Always realize that you are OURS, and we will ALWAYS ADORE YOU, and anyone you love…!" Lauren thought she could send her granddad examples of successful gay couples, or send him the documentary of *Edie & Thea*, since he could relate generationally to those women. She says, "I had all of these giant persuasive plans but in the end just decided to say, 'Thanks! Can't wait for you to meet her!'"

I was truly struck by the contradictory message that Lauren, and so many men and women like her, must feel from families who declare their love and support while maintaining the belief marriage must be between a man and a woman. What the love and support if they come with conditions?

I have no doubt that when Lauren and Jess do marry, their families—including Lauren's grandparents—will be by their sides, just as my last surviving grandparent was. I believe that even in old age the heart can achieve metamorphosis. Lauren herself admits that she is aware her family doesn't really "get" her relationship, but she is grateful that her loved ones have come out of their comfort zone for her. "I feel incredibly luckily that my family was able to see me for me and not let my relationship take away from our individual relationships." Sometimes we need to be patient with our families and let time and love work some magic. When she and Jess do get married, Lauren says, "After I send out an invite, I have done everything in my power that I can do."

For Lysa, whose wedding was featured on 2Brides2Be, her family rejected her marriage entirely, and only her brother and his baby daughter attended her wedding. Rather than focus on who was missing, Lysa spent her wedding day appreciating all the love that surrounded her. At the conclusion of her ceremony, Lysa explains, her entire bridal party surrounded her and her new wife Vanessa in a huge embrace. "We all rejoiced and jumped together; it was a moment I will never forget. I believe out of the entire night this moment impacted me most. I can only wish that every LGBT individual can feel as much support as we felt in that very moment."

Because I find her so inspiring, I asked Lysa to tell me more about her story. The photos from her wedding reveal a woman in love, a bride elated to be married. But she did not get there without a struggle, and I believe her resilience can help other women like her.

From a deeply Christian family, Lysa says that her parents found out she was a lesbian when she was a teenager. "My mother told me she would prefer to see me as a prostitute than to be with another woman. Those words will forever haunt me." She claims that her family was so distraught worrying about what others in their church would think that no one ever thought to ask Lysa how hard this was for her. She had no support at this time. She cut off contact with her family for over a year, then briefly reconciled. At this time her family accepted her now-wife Vanessa, and Lysa says things went back to normal.

Lysa says her family grew close to Vanessa. "I thought I was finally being accepted by my own family. Little did I know that they thought this was a phase and that being there for me would help get me out of it." The support of her family came to an abrupt end when Vanessa proposed to Lysa. Though her father offered his blessing, "Things changed quickly. It's like, my mother never thought this would happen. In her head, one day this torture would finally be over." As the brides began planning their wedding Lysa went to visit her mother and tell her about plans for an engagement party. Her mother told her that she would have no involvement with the wedding plans. "She told me I was not the daughter she had raised. She said she prays every day for God to bring back her sweet baby girl." Lysa had spent years trying to win her parents' acceptance, and she finally realized that she couldn't change who she was for anyone, even her own family. She told her mother, "I am that same daughter, I have not gone anywhere."

Her brother was Lysa's only family member in attendance at her wedding. He brought his baby daughter. She maintains a relationship with her family, but they do not speak often, and see each other rarely.

Of her wife's family, Lysa says, "The funny thing is, when I first met Vanessa one of the most attractive features she had was her family. Her family was so united, they loved each other and it showed. They had their differences but no matter what they were family. I could only hope that my family would one day be that way."

Lysa has come to terms with the past and looks forward to the future. "I spent so much time trying to make my family happy that I lost me." She does not regret being true to herself or making a lifelong commitment to her wife. "Although my relationship with my family is not what I would like it to be, I know that someday it will be. And if for some reason it doesn't get better, I know they are the ones missing out on my life. Our life."

I have friends whose parents claim support but who do not back it up with their behavior. One such couple involves a father who is consistently disrespectful to her fiancée, and both women wonder if they should even involve their families in their wedding at all.

Family should mean love, and when that's not the case then you have done all that you can to let them be a part of your relationship and your marriage. If there are family members on either side that you don't feel comfortable saying "I do" in front of, then don't. Your wedding is about you and your bride-to-be, and you don't owe anyone anything.

Sometimes family means the people we choose.

---

**EXPERT TIP:**

*DJ Keelez*

**What's the first thing you ask new clients?**

*What is the most important part of your wedding reception—dinner or dancing? The response to that question will help me get an idea as to the couple's expectations for the night. It also helps me lay out a proper timeline that will ensure they get to do what is most important to them.*

# Bridal Party or Not?

BEING A BRIDESMAID IN the weddings of loved ones has been some of the best memories of my adult life. Friendships, as we know, evolve over time, and zipping a childhood best friend into her wedding gown, fixing the hair of a college roommate, or handing a bouquet to a sister creates some of those "big" moments in life, the one's that we know will stay with us. My friends and family are my everything. I often say "I won the friend lottery," and it's true. Whatever life throws my way or whatever choices I make, I have a family and a gaggle of pals who have been beside me through it all. They are amazing in bad times: my sister who lives far away sends incredible notes and care packages, and a friend who lives near has washed my hair post-surgery on more than one occasion. They are amazing in good times: friends threw Sam and me an impromptu surprise engagement party. My mom and sister, a well as Sam's godmother, planned us an epic vineyard bridal shower. We all have those things in life that nag at us, the things that never work out, the bad luck and frustration. I have all of that. I have so much of that. But I also have beautiful brilliant people who love me for me. I bet you do, too. Isn't it the best?

So what happens when you have all of these people whom you love obsessively but you know that a traditional bridal party simply will not work with your wedding? Disaster? Nah. You get creative.

What if your wedding is the perfect place for bridal parties brimming with sisters, cousins, teammates, coworkers, college roommates, and kindergarten buddies? Well, you can still get creative!

- **If you and your bride-to-be both want bridal parties**: perfect. Gather your men and your women and don't worry about matching dresses or gender or numbers. Your fiancée has seven brothers and sisters you say? And she wants them all up there with her? And you're an only child with one childhood best friend and one softball[3] best friend and you want only those two up there with you? Perfect. Do it. Mix and match everyone in the photos. Have them posed haphazardly during the ceremony, or seated in a front row. There is no law that says a bridal party has to represented in the ways you've seen a hundred times—men on one side, women on the other, everyone matching down to their toes—you're free to do what works for your wedding.

- You were in a college sorority and you want your entire pledge class up there with you. Your fiancée is like, "My brother's gonna hand us the rings, otherwise, I'm good." Dilemma. What to do? Compromise.

---

3        I know, I know, softball cliché. It exists for a reason.

Just because you were in someone's wedding does not mean you're required to have them in yours. Trust me here. You can show them you love them in many other ways.

That friend lottery I won? It assured me I could not have all of those amazing girls parading down the aisle and standing up with me during the ceremony. It would have been a circus, and I wasn't going to pick and choose between them. Instead I included them in other ways: some loved ones performed readings during our ceremony, others were quoted by our officiant who interviewed them while writing our ceremony. Others still made speeches the previous night. My girlfriends all stopped by to hang out and have a glass of prosecco while I had my hair and makeup done on my wedding day, and they got to enjoy their beautiful afternoon and have fun on the venue grounds. I think it all worked out perfectly. My sister served as my maid of honor and Sam's brother was the best man. My brother was the wedding emcee and his wife read during the ceremony. Everyone had a role.

**What's your number one budget
insider-savings tip?**

*Skip wedding favors for the table and unnecessary
trinkets for attendant gifts and spring for makeup
and hair for your party! If that is too much, offer
to pay for half of the service fees as their gifts.*

**If you are planning to have bridal parties be up
front with them about your expectations.** Do you
simply need them to buy the dress of choice and
show up to the shower, bachelorette, and wedding
festivities? Or do you need them to actually plan and
pay for some of these events? Is missing the shower
a deal breaker to be your bridesmaid? Or do you use
the term loosely and really just want your best pals up
there with you on your big day? Let them know their
duties up front so no one gets in over his or her head.
And under no circumstances should you include
someone in your bridal party because you feel bad.
This is your wedding day, if everyone is not mature
enough to take their own selfish expectations out of
the equation then they are not mature enough for
weddings. Period.

When in doubt: if you're not into it, and your
bride-to-be isn't into it, skip it.

# Registry

REGISTRIES ARE COMPLETELY OUT of control these days. I mean, I would believe it if you told me you attended a wedding in which the couple registered for a car and all of the guests helped to purchase it. The new etiquette today is this: if you're getting married, you can ask for anything. I'm not promising you you'll get it, but short of registering for a new house, it seems very little is off the table.

You can register for stuff. You can register for a honeymoon. You can ask for money, literally, with a honey fund. You are no longer limited to how you ask for stuff. Remember having to choose one to three actual retailers and creating registries with them? You don't have to do that any more. You can be like, *I want place settings from Crate & Barrel, this cute little picture frame from Anthropologie, these bike helmets from Target, this lingerie from Victoria's Secret, these towels from Bed Bath & Beyond, and yes, I must have this one-of-a-kind headboard from 1stdibs.*

### Do it early

Sam and I threw an engagement party and requested no gifts. We even went so far as to let guests know where they could make donations if they felt compelled to give something. Still, there were guests who wanted to give us something, and without the guidance of a registry, they were lost. *Lost, I tell you.* Even when you think you're doing the right thing (i.e. saying "no gifts, just come, thanks!") you're still not doing the right thing if you don't tell your guests what to do. This will become a theme of wedding planning. The more information you give out the happier everyone is. No detail is too much. I promise.

I don't regret not having a registry for my engagement party. I think that would have been a bit tacky and it was too soon. We created the registry the following month, once we were ready to really get into the planning process.

### Less is more

No, really. My wife and I thought we were being so practical, registering for new dishes and flatware, things we really needed (plus the juicer I couldn't live without.) The huge toaster oven we were talked into adding to our registry, it's gorgeous and I bet it works great, but I wouldn't know because it's in a closet at my parents house two years after my wedding. You know why it's in a closet at my parents' house? Because I live in a one-bedroom apartment in New York City. There is quite literally nowhere to put a toaster oven. If you're going to a retail location I get it, that scan gun gives you power. It's tough not to scan every single item in the store like some kind of supermarket sweep, but really think it through. You can always look at everything later and remove the items that were added in the heat of the moment, but try to focus on things you really want or need. And if all you want or need is money so you can take that dream honeymoon, then register for a honeypot.

I was drunk with power in Crate & Barrel. "I must have those blue juice glasses," I ordered my wife. (No regret—I love them.) "We should really go with this knife set." We went back and forth. Which knives? What color coffee maker? Le Creuset? No, too expensive. Four non-stick pots in one box for under $200? Scan it!

### Include important items

Yes, we needed everyday dishes and juice glasses, but there were also some picture frames that I knew would look beautiful holding our wedding photos, and though our apartment was no place for crystal stemware, we knew we would want the good stuff someday. "Meh," we agreed, "Let's add it to the list and if nobody gets it, no big deal." Now we have a set of stunning, classic, crystal stemware that will not come out of its box until we live in a home big enough to give those glasses the life they deserve. It's okay to choose items that are special or even offbeat.

Its okay to choose things that you think are crazy expensive, but also be sure to add things that are affordable. It's important to run the gamut. What's worse than going on a registry with a number in mind only to find that everything available is double the price?

**Hot tip:** queen of etiquette Martha Stewart says we shouldn't put registry information on the invitations, and I'm inclined to agree with her. I suggest you use your website. Or let family spread the word. Or, if you're having a bridal shower, include the information on those invitations.

In the registry world of anything goes, you need only do a little research on what it is you really want and chances are, there's a way to get it.

Keep this in mind: if you're registering for material items, you may find that you've received only partial sets of your items. This might mean that post-wedding you're going to need to spend an extra $500 for your remaining pillow shams and dinner plates. If you want complete sets make sure you budget for them. You'll likely get these items at a discount, but they can still add up.

# The Wedding Regimen

THE TWO MOST ANNOYING wedding traditions: spending less and eating less.

### Shedding for the wedding

I can't diet. This will haunt me as I get older, but for three decades I've managed to find great happiness in spite of this. My wife and I tried to cut down as the months turned to weeks. She lost weight, but I stayed pretty much the same. I did tone up, which is all I really worried about. I didn't need to lose twenty pounds and I didn't want to. This notion women have that once there's a ring on their finger they'll finally be able to achieve the body that's been evading them their whole lives—that's a farce. If you're not going to be realistic then you're going to be disappointed.

The best way to slim down your bod and bulk up your wallet involves more meals at home. While the wedding countdown is a celebratory time with lots of happy hour dates and dining out, make a commitment to do less of this. Maybe you go out for dinner one night a weekend, and if you're a slave to delivery, like me, then aim to cook dinner at least four nights a week. This means you're spending less money and eating healthier portions.

That gym membership that's been sucking money out of your bank account each month? Start using it. You'll love how a little cardio helps melt away that wedding stress. Working on a playlist for the wedding? Try out new music during your circuit training workouts. You're not only going to look better, you're going to feel better, too.

And another thing. Married women warned me that I would drop some weight the last week before my wedding. "Impossible," I told them, "I don't drop weight." Well, my boobs shrank that final week. They all but disappeared. Apparently that is how I *drop weight*. So if possible, schedule a final fitting for the week of the wedding, and be prepared for a couple of pounds to disappear.

EXPERT TIP:

*Kathryn Conover, Gown Designer*

**What's your number one budget insider-savings tip?**

*Get to your fitness goal and ideal size before you begin your fittings. Bring various undergarments to your first fitting to try before you start your fittings. Once you start your fittings, do them once a month.*

### *Tips for saving money*

*Wedding related*

Find a photographer who will include an engagement shoot with the cost of your wedding package. You can use photos from this shoot for your save-the-dates, and you get to learn how it feels to pose for your photographer.

Make budget-conscious rental decisions. If you choose white linens you can save a ton of money, and dressing up the palette is a no-brainer, thanks to Pinterest and your wedding vendors.

Start shopping early. Need an outfit for the rehearsal dinner? A perfect bowtie for the wedding day? The sooner you start looking for these things the more likely you are to find deals.

Talk to your venue and/or wedding planner about their preferred vendors. Often those vendors have the best pricing options.

Talk to your vendors about payment plans and cash options which can help save you money.

No impulse buys. Thought you loved a pair of shoes that were $500 and final sale? Think again. Know what you want and seek it out. Unless you're certain about those shoes, keep looking.

*Everyday changes*

Make your own coffee. I know, I love paying someone to make my coffee, but between you and your fiancée, you can stash away more than twenty dollars a week if you switch to at-home brew.

Rather than your standing Saturday movie date, stay in. Skip the expensive movie tickets and the pricey snacks that come with it, and stay home, pop some corn, and rent a movie. If you start limiting these nights out you'll see savings in no time.

Give up booze. I know, this is crazy, but maybe take one month, like January, and go dry for a few weeks. You'll feel better, look better, and if you're usually drinking fifteen dollar cocktails a couple times a week, your wallet will thank you.

No more gift giving. You and your fiancée are planning a wedding. You don't need to be showering each other with gifts, everyone else is gonna do that. This Christmas exchange stocking stuffers, or stick to sweet homemade gifts for Hanukah. You'll have a fun (or funny) memory and you won't waste money.

# Get (and Keep) Everyone Excited

**T**HERE'S AN AGE WE all reach when our lives feel like this: eat, sleep, work, wedding. Suddenly everyone you know is engaged, every weekend it's a party or a shower or a bachelorette and you're exhausted, and of course, broke. But you want everyone to get excited when it's your turn, right?

Here's the secret. Make your wedding about you and your bride, but plan events and moments that will get all of your loved ones excited to celebrate with you. Don't ask for too much, and don't be afraid to give a little. Examples: my wife and I wanted an engagement party to kick off the months of celebration ahead, but we weren't after gifts or a formal affair. We had the party in a candlelit bar in Brooklyn and requested no gifts. We did, however, share information on our chosen charity to anyone interested in making a donation.

We also wanted a big bridal shower out on a vineyard on the North Fork of Long Island—one of our favorite places to visit in summer. Because most of our friends lived in New York City, we rented a party bus to provide transportation and ensure everyone could not only attend, but have a good time.

We asked many of our guests to stay in cabins during our wedding weekend, and, as you know, cabin life is not for everyone. We spent the entire night before our guests arrived making over sixty beds, and leaving our friends' favorite spirits in their space to make everyone a bit more comfortable. By making the cabins a bit more comfortable and leaving a bounty of booze for their enjoyment, we knew they would have fun from the moment they arrived until they were puking by the bonfire at the after-party.

Guests will not forget these thoughtful details. Something we still hear, over two years after our wedding, is this: "you thought of everything."

Our excited energy and celebratory spirit was contagious, it was impossible not to have fun.

EXPERT TIP:

*Breck Hofstedder, Sesame Letterpress*

### What's the biggest mistake you see brides making?

*Second-guessing themselves! I think this is the greatest mistake brides make and it happens all the time. We are finding more and more that brides get overwhelmed by options and try to incorporate all these ideas, then stray too far from their original preferences and get stressed out, second-guessing everything. Ninety-nine percent of the time, they circle back and go with their initial idea and are relieved. Trust your instincts and if you do start to doubt yourself, ask your stationer for his/her opinion. They can help you pick and choose which trend works with the style you are going for and which might take the design too far away from it.*

## Ask for Help

Loved ones want to help. My wife and I could not give up control and asked for very little help, but persistent friends and family managed to break us, providing invaluable assistance. They key is to ask for help but be flexible. Believe me, I know that the only way to do something right is to do it yourself, but will it really kill you to have your mom throw some Advil and pretzels into the welcome bags? Nah.

My wife and I bought cases of water bottles and printed our own labels for them. Sam was a beast, eyeing me, my mom, and my sister to be sure we were lining those labels up precisely. God forbid our label was uneven, she wanted to toss the bottle into the "no" pile. Know what happened? They quit. We had to label them ourselves because WaterBottleZilla couldn't control herself. Did any of our guests care in the slightest about the wedding water? Nope.

### Be Nice to Your Bridal Party

Is it really imperative that your bridesmaids all have the same chignon in their hair, the same Essie color on their fingernails, and the same exact pair of stilettos pinching their toes? Nobody likes a bridezilla. Although mix-matched bridal parties are in, if your dream is to have your girls all in the same eggplant pillar dress, go for it, but give them a little freedom with the rest of their styling. And if you want everyone in hair and makeup, then covering some of that cost makes for a great gift to your bridesmaids.

I've been in bridal parties where we as a group were responsible for planning showers, bachelorette parties, and organizing specific wedding details. I've also been in bridal parties where my only job was to show up to my hair appointment on time and be ready for pictures. Every bride is different, so be up front with your bridal party about your needs. Are they responsible for throwing and funding your bridal shower? Let them know this. Do you want them to fly to Vegas for your bach? Let them know—and keep in mind that it's okay if someone has to skip an event here or there. I had very dear friends miss my engagement party or wedding shower, and it's okay to be disappointed, but it's not okay to let it ruin your good time.

### Choose Vendors You Like

I'm serious. Wedding planning is not your job, you don't have to play nice with colleagues you can't stand. Surrounding yourself with positive, hardworking vendors whom you actually like being around will make wedding planning that much easier. Of course you can't always tell when you hire them that your wedding planner might stop answering your emails weeks before your wedding, but use your best judgment early on. If someone rubs you the wrong way on your first meeting, trust that instinct. That instinct was what stopped us from wasting our time (and money) on vendors with whom we didn't jive.

EXPERT TIP:

*Meg Nobile, Florist & Designer, That Time Events*

**What's the most important detail brides should look for when choosing their florist?**

*I would say that your styles align, not only floral styles, but personal style, too. Meet and get to know each other. If you believe in using local and seasonal flowers, so should your florist. You will be working with your florist on something personal to you, so feel comfortable in their company. Lastly, make sure he or she is a good listener and they aren't just going to do what they prefer—it's your wedding after all!*

### Know What's Important

Yes, I do mean that marrying the love of your life matters and you should focus on that, but it's okay to get super serious about having the perfect band at your wedding. That was my main focus. My wife wanted incredible food. These two items became top priorities for us. We designed a one-of-a kind menu based on our favorite foods, and we hired a kick-ass rock band that played my favorite classics. Choose the ways in which you're willing to stretch your budget and the ways in which you can save. It's okay to say "no" to a few items on your wish list, as long as they're not going to make or break your wedding day mood. My wife really, really wanted to hang a chandelier in our reception space, but the cost was simply too high. We skipped it, and a few years later, the venue now has a stunning permanent chandelier. Are we a little jealous of their upgrades? Sure. Would a chandelier have made our wedding any better than it was? Nope.

### Be Prepared

Planning a wedding weekend in a rustic, outdoor venue was a major gamble. If the weather was great our wedding could be incredible. If it rained the most expensive weekend of our lives—and the one we got to spend with all of our family and friends— could be a disaster. Having a realistic plan B kept me feeling positive. Instead of kickball and swimming the day of our wedding, rain would mean board games and cocktails by the fire in the covered dining pavilion. Once I knew this was the plan I could breathe a little easier. Was I still a mess, obsessively checking the weather every day for weeks leading up to my wedding? Of course, but I wasn't going to let anything ruin our celebration.

### Maintain a Sense of Humor

Things go wrong. You might forget the welcome bags in your garage. You might get a zit. It might rain. I don't even remember the little things that went wrong at my wedding. Those are not the details that will stick with you—or your guests—if you don't focus on them. If you're in hysterics and obsessing over your ruined wedding because the makeup artist forgot your false eyelashes, then that's what you'll remember. Go with the flow. Marriage isn't perfect. Weddings aren't either. It's all in how you perceive it.

### Ask a Guest

I polled a few two-bride wedding guests to ask them their favorite and least-favorite wedding elements. Bridesmaid Emma admitted that her least favorite part of a wedding is watching the couples-only dances. She also believes that all guests should get a plus one, even if they're single. Alexa Leigh, my cousin and a teenage guest at my own wedding, admits that sometimes it's hard to pay attention during the ceremony. She loves the celebratory mood, however, and getting together with family. I was not surprised to hear that she loves the open bar, too.

### Enjoy the Planning

The wedding is a moment in your life that will fly by. I still cannot believe my wedding is over and I've been married over two years. But I remember the fun of dress shopping, and the delicious cake-tasting my wife and I enjoyed at Milk Bar in Brooklyn. I loved choosing our favorite wines to serve at our wedding, and meeting with our florist and event designer to share images and ideas. My wife and I enjoyed all of it, and of course we got into arguments. We are a couple who bickers constantly, and her OCD while I stuffed invitation envelopes almost resulted in a homicidal bride, but I look back on wedding planning as one of the best years of our lives together. Being engaged was a blast. Enjoy it. It goes fast.

EXPERT TIP:

Stephanie Karvellas-Baynton, Owner & Venue Coordinator at Cedar Lakes Estate

### What's the biggest mistake you see brides making?

*Sweating the small stuff. Brides need to remember what the day—or weekend—is all about. When you stress over the less impactful details, you waste time and energy that could be spent soaking in the fun planning process and the focus on the marriage itself!*

# PART THREE

## The Commotion

A WEDDING IS NEVER *just* a wedding. There are so many other events and details that go into your wedding. Your engagement, therefore, is a time in your life you want to look back on with great joy. You'll remember the friends who stepped up to celebrate this special time in your life, and you'll appreciate the moments with your fiancée as you plan to become wife and wife.

There are occasions and milestones to be enjoyed, but there's also myriad advice you'll receive—both solicited and not—from your loved ones. There's etiquette to learn and bachelorette parties to plan. It's not frequent in life that we get these festive periods, so it's important to do only what feels right for you. Focus on what matters most and you will look back on your engagement and wedding planning as one of the best times in your lives.

# Bachelorette Party

I'M A DRINKER AND a bitch so I'm comfortable being honest when I say I'm not big into joint bachelorette parties. I mean, it goes against the very nature of bachelorette parties. It's basically just a group trip. I am also prone to inappropriate behavior. I spent an entire day of my New Orleans bachelorette party nude in a pool bumming cigs from guys whose penises were flopping about. I screamed at strangers to get into the water and made up names for all of them. My sister, in an attempt to force me back to our rental, took my top and other personal belongings—including my ID and cash—home with her. Well, the joke was on her because I somehow ended up in the French quarter wearing only wet jean shorts and a tank top my best friend had made that read "Blame it on My Wild Heart" on the front and "Laura Leigh's New Orleans Bachelorette August 2013" on the back. I carried my bikini around in a plastic bag and got denied entrance to a club because I was without identification. "I was probably your babysitter," I argued with the young bouncer. My remaining friends and I sauntered over to our hotspot, a small gay bar we'd been frequenting all weekend. They served me, in spite of my lack of ID, money, and dignity.

Anyway, I digress. I am a firm believer that a bachelorette party should be an all-out shitshow. I know I am, perhaps, in the minority. I've heard there are women who go to the spa and split a bottle of wine at dinner. Now, married and tame, that sounds like heaven, but I was going somewhere wild for my bachelorette party, less a fiancée, and with an additional fifteen fabulous friends in tow, both male and female. Sam flew cross-country to Vegas with her nearest and dearest while I headed south. That's right, we chose the same weekend. Guess what? It was a genius move.

The truth is it's a bit scary imagining your fiancée misbehaving in Las Vegas with her friends cheering her on. It's less scary if you're busy misbehaving in New Orleans with your friends cheering you on. Sam and I checked in with each other during the course of our bachelorette trips, but we otherwise resolved to talking when we both made it back to New York.

I knew I was asking a lot of my friends to have them: A) take off work for a long weekend and B) fly. Most of my friends' bachelorettes have been in locations within driving distance and I knew I was being greedy. I made sure every single person I invited knew there would be no ill will if they chose not to come. I was shocked when so many of my friends excitedly announced they were on board, and I tried to help curb costs by paying for a chunk of our rental and purchasing some groceries for the house, but I am unbelievably lucky to have a sister and friends who sought to make me happy.

If a weekend in a far-flung locale is your idea of a good time too, then get a plan going early on. Your friends may need a few months to make it happen. If it's Vegas or bust but none of your friends can go, then downsize to something local. Keep in mind that what matters most is not where you are, it's who you're with. If you're like me and you are inviting a bunch of friends, figure out dates that work for you then send out the calendar and let everyone fill in the dates that also work for them. Choose the days that work for the most people.

If you don't want to make a trip out of it, you don't need to. There's nothing wrong with having a bachelorette party your way. I did not wear a sash or a tiara. I'm not that kind of gal. I simply traipsed all over NOLA with my pals and drank no small amount of liquor. Would you rather go get a mani/pedi with your best friends than drink wine on your couch all night? Do it. Maybe you live in Boston and can't remember the last time you went on a bar crawl down Boylston Street. Get some T-shirts printed and pick a date! There is no right or wrong way to have a bachelorette party but trust me—you should have one. It's a great opportunity to have some time with your best pals before you inevitably do almost everything ever with your wife.

It's worth noting that my wife and I both know bits and pieces of what went on at our bachelorette weekends, but we chose not to share in-depth. I have it on good authority that she and her friends ate wings at the strip club where they got a whole bunch of lap dances—she was traveling with all straight girls and two guys, mind you—and they also flooded a hotel room. Her best friend was a club promoter in Vegas at the time, and sometimes I'm a teeny bit envious that I missed that epic trip. However, I wouldn't trade my New Orleans fun for anything.

My friends and I often reminisce about our bachelor and bachelorette celebrations. The key, I believe, is this truth that as we grow older and we get married and maybe start families of our own, the quality of the time with our friends diminishes. This is the natural course of things, so we have to make better efforts to spend time together. The pre-wedding raucous bachelorette celebration can be a throwback to your college days, or it can usher in a new era of better behavior. Whatever you and your friends are into, do it together, in the name of one last fling before the ring.

# Bridal Shower

**O**KAY SO YOU KNOW my opinion on bachelorette parties, but guess what—the best part of being a lesbian couple is having a bridal shower! (Okay it might not be the *best* part but it's awesome.)

Let's just come right out and say it: showers can be boring. Yours doesn't have to be. Besides, you know what I always say: do whatever you want. Wanna have a bridal shower in your favorite sports bar? Why not? Wanna avoid playing toilet paper bride and other embarrassing games, skip 'em. This is your shower and you should do it your way.

Since there are two of you there's plenty of ways to keep those shower-game purists happy. You know that game where the bridesmaids ask the groom a bunch of questions and then they put the bride in the hot seat and ask her what his answers are? You can play this together! Hooray!

I haven't been to many showers where lingerie is on the agenda, so if you're bashful on that front, don't be. By now you'll have a wedding registry and when your friends shower you and your bride, it will likely be with stemless wine glasses and tea kettles.

Some tips and advice. Often the brides are not throwing their own shower, which means your moms or bridesmaids or other loved ones are pooling their time and money to throw you a shower. Even if you don't want one. Try to be a good sport and remember that there are some wedding elements that are more for our families than for us. If you want a shower, meanwhile, and don't have anyone to throw it for you, go ahead and ask your bridesmaids or best pals. I've thrown showers at home with prosecco and quiche, and I've attended showers at restaurants, bars, godmother's homes, the list goes on. Two brides mean two sets of parents-of-the-bride, so if your moms are going head to head, now is a good time to invest in your future and ask them to team up and work together. I know, this can be a dangerous game, but you might be surprised at how well it works out.

Because my wife's mother was gone, we went into our wedding planning process a little ruthless. Sam spent her whole life imagining wedding planning with her mom, and without her there many of the traditions lost their allure. Because most of my family lives on Long Island and we love the North Fork, we decided we wanted a vineyard bridal shower. This would come at an expense, we knew, and there was also the fact that most of our friends live in New York City. We asked my mom and Sam's godmother to team up and plan the shower. They didn't see eye-to-eye on every detail, but together they planned a beautiful day that made us feel like the luckiest girls in the world. I set a strict "no game" rule, but we did get roped into one round of bridal bingo. Sam and I did our part by renting a party bus to transport us and our friends, and once the vineyard beauty was over, well, all bets were off. I also made a speech after a few glasses of chardonnay that involved holding up my baby niece and yelling the world "lesbian."

I hate opening gifts in front of people. Nothing about it feels right, but we went ahead and did it. Remember, some of these traditions are to make other people happy, and you may not realize that your aunt Barbara really wants to see you open that salad spinner. I rushed through a little bit, but I really enjoyed the day in its entirety. It was another great day with my loved ones, and this event was strictly women, which was fabulous all on its own.

- You can make invitations online or buy them at your local party store. In fact, you can get just about everything you'll need for a shower there.
- Take this opportunity to thank the women in your lives for being so special. Maybe a corsage or bouquets for moms or grandmas.
- Make sure you delegate someone to keep track of your gifts. You want to know who got you what. You're not only going to need to send out thank-you cards after the shower, but the gift list is good to have around for the future when you're wondering what to spend on the weddings of your past guests.
- The shower is a good time for your favorite informal themes. If there's something you love to do together as a couple that wouldn't lend itself to the wedding day, use it for your shower. Maybe you met over a cup of tea and want a high-tea party, or you met at summer camp and want a camp theme complete with friendship bracelets. Or maybe you just love mimosas and muffins and chatting with your girlfriends.

### Games

- Toilet paper bride (makes for good photos): you split your guests into teams and they each get a few roles of toilet paper. Set the time for five minutes and watch as they make a wedding gown on one lucky guest. You and your bride get to vote on the winner.
- Bridal bingo.

- Twenty questions: you can play one at a time or take turns answering. Again, this is especially fun since you're both present.
- Wedding wishes: each guest writes a wish for the couple. You can turn these into a scrapbook, ornaments, or even magnets to use in daily life.
- Recipes: have each guest write their favorite recipe on a card and turn it into a book. If you feel so inclined, print a copy for every guest.
- Guess her age: hang up about a dozen photos of you and your bride from various ages and have your guests guess your ages in each photo. Whoever gets the most right wins.
- Movie quotes: put up a poster board with quotes from famous love stories. Guests will each guess what movie the quotes are from and write them down. Read through them at the end. Whoever gets the most right wins.

Don't forget—you need prizes for all the winners!

# Gifts & Gratuity

I T'S CUSTOMARY TO GIVE your bridal party gifts the night before or day of your wedding. If you have friends giving readings or performing rituals during your ceremony, it's nice to show your thanks for them, too, and don't forget your parents. These gifts don't need to be a huge expense. Remember how I decided to forego a bridal party because I have too many wonderful friends? I bought them all simple beaded bracelets with notes of thanks. Sam made her group customized Converse sneakers, and we went with more traditional gifts for our parents like engraved handkerchiefs and artwork.

If you're not sure what to get your bridal party, footing the bill for some or all of their hair and makeup costs is always a classy move. If you're just having a maid of honor like I did, maybe you can buy her dress. I did that for my sister and she appreciated the gesture (and I'm still waiting to borrow it).

For guys there's always the gift of a professional shave, and gifts like a rare bottle of liquor or theater tickets can be the perfect personal gesture.

You'll also want to tip your vendors. You can find many gratuity suggestions online through sites like The Knot or Brides, but you can also tip based on your experience and level of service. Did your wedding planner go over and above? Did your DJ give you an extra thirty minutes? Don't let these moves go unnoticed. If the stress of tipping everyone the day of your wedding feels like too much, here are two great options:

Mail them a thank-you after the wedding. A handwritten note with a gift or gratuity is always appreciated, and you'll be able to reflect after the fact.

Put a bridesmaid or a brother in charge of the envelopes. As a teenager I worked as a waitress at a country club, and there was nothing better than a groomsmen finding me before the wedding to hand me a white envelope with cash in it. It put me in a great mood for the rest of the evening and, if I'm being honest, I worked a little harder.

*Plan ahead so the gratuity is part of your budget, and check your vendor contracts. Some venues include gratuity for their wait staff, for instance, so you may have already tipped them and don't know it yet.

## *Same-Sex Wedding Etiquette*

*\*Tear this page out and give it to an Aunt who doesn't "get it," or a friend whose boyfriend "doesn't really know any lesbians."*

Great news! Same-sex wedding etiquette differs very little from wedding etiquette in general.

I'm not someone who is easily offended, especially by people who are enthusiastic and supportive.

> *Example: "I am so excited to go to a lesbian wedding!"*

This phrase was something I heard many times while wedding planning. Rather than try to correct every offender, I focused instead on the positive side of what they were telling me. Guests were truly looking forward to my wedding, *Hooray.* This is not always the case, and I loved all of the build-up for the big wedding weekend. I loved all of the politically incorrect fervor, of which there was plenty. I loved, loved, loved it all. Alas, not all same-sex couples are as mellow with this sort of talk. Let me be clear, I've offended no small handful of people in my life. Lest you do the same, here are a few pointers for same-sex wedding guests.

**First**: gay couples do not plan gay weddings. We just plan weddings. If we're asking you to witness this then we're also asking for a degree of respect for our marriage.

If you're not on the best-bud level of comfort with the brides, then don't say anything that can be construed as sexist, homophobic, or in any way offensive. If you're wondering if you should ask, don't. If you're not sure how the brides will receive your hilarious joke about which one's the groom, don't tell it. Basically, if you're not certain, don't say it. This is a good rule of thumb. That being said, even if you are best buds with the brides, don't be the drunk guy who jokingly toasts, "Cheers to the dykes!"

If you're dying to know what the bride's father thinks of her getting hitched to a chick, assume that if he's present he's on board, so no need to confront any family members on how they are "coping" with having a gay kid. If family members are visibly missing, the wedding is not a good time to ask the bride about it.

So to recap: if her family is present—avoid this topic. If her family is not—avoid this topic.

> *Example: "It's so great that your parents are cool with all of this."*

My parents are fine. Marrying me off to a hard-working, organized girl with a few bucks in the bank and a 100 percent dedication to spoiling me with love and happiness does not keep my parents up at night.

If you want to know what the brides are wearing, ask. You don't need to say it like this, "So you're both wearing dresses? That's crazy." You can just say, "Do you know what you're wearing yet?" Most brides will either be excited to talk about her wedding day look, or she's keeping it a secret. Wanna know who walks down the aisle? If you don't know how to ask this without being offensive then wait to find out at the wedding. Safe questions always begin with, "Do you know what your ceremony processional is going to be like?" There are ways to ask questions without making the brides feel like their wedding is an oddity.

Basically, don't be a dick. Don't burn the place down. Don't get black-out drunk (unless it's that kind of party, which my wedding certainly was) and for the love of God do not forget a card. And if you really want to go above and beyond as a guest at a lesbian wedding, get a card specifically for two brides. This gesture will not go unnoticed.

# When All Else Fails: My Five Pearls of Wisdom

SINCE PLANNING MY OWN wedding and taking my relationship so nauseatingly public, I've learned how remarkably easy it is to relate to each other. I'm in a same-sex relationship and I live in New York, but that doesn't mean that I can't relate to every other girl out there who is planning a wedding of her own. Any of us who have planned or are now planning a wedding knows that we all face similar challenges during a time that is both exciting and stressful. I've amassed some advice that I believe is pretty solid.

Here are my **top five** little tiny pearls of wedding planning wisdom. You've seen this earlier in the book, but I'm repeating them because they're important:

- Create a new email address for your wedding. You'll be *so* glad you did this. I thought I was being cute and clever when I came up with 2brides2be, which began as an email address before I had the idea for a blog and then the site you see today. Keeping our wedding emails out of our individual inboxes kept us organized without getting us overwhelmed.

- Don't hire a single vendor that you don't connect with. I know the word "connect" can be so ridiculous. I'm not one to sit down for coffee with plans to become besties with my potential photographer, but I'm glad that my wife and I went with our instincts on who to work with. Planning our wedding was a blast, in part because we genuinely enjoyed everyone who helped make it happen.

- Don't be afraid to ask for help. Ya know when you read a wedding blog and the bride gushes about her sister-in-law who baked the wedding cake and six pies for the dessert table, or the great-aunt who sewed burlap table runners and you're thinking, *Seriously*? I have no one in my life that can build a chuppah or bake dessert for 175 people, but my friends and family did help in other ways. Sam and I did not have a traditional wedding party, so we found various elements with which to include our loved ones. We had friends helping us make beds in the cabins where many of our guests were staying, and we employed my mom to help us make gift bags. We actually didn't ask for enough outside help, and I wish we had. Loved ones want to be involved and most will be willing to lend a hand. (Anyone who isn't will probably let you know!)

- Take your ceremony seriously! Don't laugh or roll your eyes because this seems *so* obvious. When planning our ceremony I was terrified at the thought of making everyone sit there and pay attention to such intimate moments between us. I am so glad that we hired a professional celebrant and I am glad that we asked our friends and family to gather with us. Who cares if your ceremony is a little long? We gave our guests cocktails and knew they would sit still for a little while! I know a major wedding trend right now is for couples to ask a friend to officiate their wedding. Some of my own friends have done this and it made for such a personal and enjoyable ceremony. I do not recommend asking a friend who has never done anything like this, but I do think this is an especially excellent idea if you have a friend or relative who has previously performed a ceremony, and even better if you love your priest or rabbi, if your mom's best friend is a minister, or if you find yourself in some other similar situation. This is your wedding day, and it's okay to gather your guests to witness a beautiful, well-planned ceremony. My wife and I were married by a seasoned pro who knew how to handle such an important occasion. Take the ceremony seriously and allow it to be special.

- Sit down and discuss the wedding of your dreams with your fiancée. You cannot plan a wedding trying to make everyone else happy. If you attempt to do that, you will just end up making yourselves unhappy. Sam and I didn't want to spend our entire wedding day having our hair and makeup done, so we had a big brunch followed by kegs and kickball. We got to enjoy our whole day with family and friends. Plan the wedding you really want and your loved ones will be honored to celebrate with you, even if they think kickball on your wedding day is nuts.

If you're not planning a wedding and you're going to like, a thousand this year, here are only two tiny things to remember:

- Don't complain to the bride. If you have a concern or a complaint, find someone else— anyone else—to share it with.
- Bring a card. If you're not giving a gift for any reason, at least write a nice card. We had friends who went out of their way to find cards on Etsy that were meant for two brides, and those are special keepsakes. I won't forget that they did that, and I've since made it a point to do the same myself. (This has become much easier this past year as more and more mainstream card companies roll out same-sex greeting cards.)

EXPERT TIP:

*Jill Hammelman, Hair Design*

**What's the biggest mistake you see brides making?**

*A lot of brides are trying to please their mother or mother-in-law by wearing their hair up or with traditional headpieces or styles. In the end it's your day and you are the star of the show. Do what makes you happy.*

# PART FOUR

## The Ceremony

I DON'T EVER WANT brides to overlook their wedding ceremony. It's why your family and friends have gathered. It's your time to make vows to each other in front of the people you love, those that will be there for the ups and downs ahead in your marriage. Go ahead and make it matter.

This might be the most solemn moment you've shared publicly. Loved ones may be involved in your readings or rituals. You will kiss—maybe for the first time—in front of family and friends. By the end of your ceremony you will be married, and you want you, your bride, and your guests to remember these moments as beautiful.

# Finding an Officiant

LIKE AN ELECTED POLITICIAN'S, my views on officiants have evolved over time. I used to be a steadfast believer in "professionals only." I simply could not imagine that a friend or loved one could actually do the job correctly. Then I attended weddings with loved ones leading the proceedings. One friend who was officiating asked many of us guests to send her some thoughts on the bride and groom. She ended up quoting me in the ceremony, so, ya know, I'm a bit of a believer. Enough patting myself on the back. The point is that I was touched by these ceremonies.

I've also attended weddings officiated by both a priest and a rabbi. Sam and I hired a Master Life-Cycle Celebrant® and Interfaith Minister for our wedding, and I'm glad we did. They made it really easy for us. We were able to look at photos and read about the various celebrants before choosing who to meet with and eventually, who was right for our wedding.

Start by talking to trusted loved ones. A conversation with an aunt led us to The Celebrant Foundation and Institute. Once they've shared their suggestions, you can speak to clergymen or members of your house of worship if you're looking to go in that direction. If friends offer—even if it sounds like a great idea—thank them and tell them you'll think about it. It never hurts to sleep on it and come up with what works best for you and your future wife.

You know I am adamant about the ceremony being the most important aspect of the wedding, and it's important to feel comfortable with the person marrying you. You're going to be sharing intimate details about your life with them. They'll likely be seeing your vows before anyone else. Their job is to tell your story in a beautiful way and make you feel secure in the process. Of course, a same-sex wedding gives the ceremony added impact. We have our rights, but what we're doing is a little different, and it's important to have an officiant who can handle this gracefully.

A good way to think about what kind of officiant you want is to consider the tone of your ceremony. Do you want there to be lots of laughs? Then maybe your hilarious college roommate is, in fact, the right one for the job. Do you want your faith at the forefront, or do you want a variety, in which case a professional celebrant might be your best fit.

EXPERT TIP:

*Elizabeth Phaire, Master Life-Cycle Celebrant® and Interfaith Minister*

**What's the most important detail brides should look for when choosing their officiant?**

*The most important detail brides should look for is professional training. Is the officiant educated in the art of crafting personalized ceremony for couples who come from different cultures and faiths? Do they have experience working with same-sex couples?*

*For this reason, I recommend that couples look for an officiant who is also a certified Life-Cycle Celebrant®. With a Life-Cycle Celebrant®, the couple can be assured that their ceremony will be crafted with attentiveness, care, and creativity. They will be expertly guided through the entire planning process and their unique ceremony needs will be taken into account. Where they are unsure they can rely on their celebrant's knowledge. The celebrant will work with their ideas and show the best way to implement them, also provide excellent options and resources. Their ceremony will be beautifully personalized to include readings, music, and ritual elements that are meaningful to them as a couple, and will incorporate the story of their love journey. Prior to the wedding day they get to read the script and give feedback to ensure that the ceremony is exactly as they want it to be.*

### Some tips

- Don't hire anyone you haven't met in person. Your officiant is going to be marrying you. You want to be sure you're comfortable with their mannerisms, facial expressions, and voice. If you and your fiancée are going to giggle at his lisp then this guy may not be right for your wedding day. You'll also get a feel for their vibe and how the three of you are going to interact together.

- Take it seriously. If you're worried that having your brother officiate will result in a goofy ceremony, then go with a pro. Sam and I are notoriously good at dodging all things serious, so we knew we wanted an officiant who would keep us on-task and maintain the meaningful focus of our ceremony. My brother's quips really shined in his role as emcee.

- You can have more than one. If you want officiants that represent your different religious or cultural upbringings, or you would like a sister-brother team to officiate, let them share the job of marrying you.

- Choose an officiant who is flexible. You want someone who is going to guide you, not force you to partake in rituals that don't interest you, or who is going to speak words that don't feel authentic to you. We went back and forth with our celebrant to decide what words sounded best to declare us as married. She made great suggestions and was open to our ideas and in the end, she did what worked best for us (which was: "I now pronounce you wife and wife").

- In the end, you should choose the person that feels right to you and your bride-to-be. Just because Uncle John insists that his best friend is a minster does not mean you have to be persuaded. Trust yourselves.

Designing our ceremony with our officiant was such a wonderful part of our planning process. It was such a joy going through the drafts, reading the rituals we'd chosen, and even seeing what loved ones had to say about us. It's so worth taking the time to design the ceremony that's right for you.

### *Readings and rituals*

Once you have chosen an officiant they will certainly be available to help you choose your rituals and readings for your ceremony, but you might already have some ideas of your own, which is great.

Our officiant created a draft for our wedding that included the story of us; a tribute to Sam's mom, Penny; readings of our choice; and remarks from some of our family and friends. Sam and I enjoyed choosing our ceremony readings almost as much as we enjoyed listening to them at our wedding. A few of them were no-brainers, while others we had to work to find. Our officiant helped us with this by providing us with examples. Don't be afraid to ask yours for suggestions. Many ceremonies include prayer or blessings, and while our ceremony was not religious, we did include an Irish blessing. Our readings were certainly atypical, but that's us!

Our first reading, given by Sam's Aunt Lisa was *A Lovely Love Story* by Edward Monkton. This story is about two unlikely companions, dinosaurs, who find love. We made both dinosaurs female in our version. Next, my dear friend Kate read an entry from my journal, which I wrote on January 19, 2005, when I was nineteen years old. This was maybe the strangest choice, but it outlined both my fear of falling in love with Sam and my fear of not being with her. If I was going to showcase my vulnerability and have a wedding ceremony witnessed by family and friends, then I was going all the way. Next, our sister-in-law Jaine read the lyrics to "Hum Along" by Ludo, a favorite song of ours from early in our relationship. The ending is about pirates and bushwacking and fairytales. We like that sort of thing.

Our final reading was read by Sam's friend Chris, who read an Irish blessing, "May the Road Rise Up to Meet You," which paid homage to my heritage.

Our readers were excellent and our readings really meant something to us, which made them both a special and indispensable element of our wedding ceremony.

You might read through religious text to find readings that fit your ceremony, or maybe scour a book of beloved poems. You can have your two best friends read duet lyrics, or recite lines from a film or a play. Get creative and have fun with this. Your ceremony is something of a performance, and it's about your relationship, so don't be afraid to think outside the box.

Rituals are another way to make your ceremony your own. Maybe your ceremony is on a beach and you would like to do a sand ritual. Maybe you're going to be a stepmom and you'd like to do a handfasting ritual to bind you together as a family. You can light a unity candle, or pass your rings around for your guests to warm with their hands. Choose only those rituals that feel meaningful to you, and don't do too many, otherwise guests will lose interest and each element may lose relevance.

To open our ceremony, Sam lit a candle in memory of her mother while our officiant spoke a few words. The candle would remain lit through the evening. Our handfasting represented our physical and spiritual connection as a couple, now bound through marriage. You can drink from the same glass of wine during your ceremony, release doves or butterflies, even cast a stone into a body of water. There are many possible rituals that might have meaning for you and your bride, and if not, there's no requirement that you do any. For some couples, exchanging rings and vows is ritual enough.

EXPERT TIP:

*Elizabeth Phaire, Master Life-Cycle Celebrant® and Interfaith Minister*

**Anything you steer couples away from?**

*I steer couples away from including too many readings and unity rituals, especially unity rituals that would be redundant. I'm talking about something like four readings and five unity rituals. The typical length of ceremony is half an hour, though some couples opt for a longer ceremony which can include more elements. There are so many beautiful options that it can be hard for some couples to choose just a few! They may think* **the more the better,** *but too many rituals and readings can actually dilute the meaning of them. For a half-hour ceremony, at most there should be a total of five rituals and readings, combined.*

### Reading and ritual suggestions

- If you really would prefer a brief ceremony, you can ask your officiant to open with a few chosen words, perhaps even a line from your favorite movie, to get things started. From there you can skip everything else, if you choose to.
- If you're tempted not to go for anything too obvious, try to explore similar options. Maybe you're thinking of Elizabeth Barrett Browning's, "How Do I Love Thee?" or maybe Corinthians 13:4-8 which begins "love is patient, love is kind." These are not bad suggestions, but you can also

explore the work of your favorite author. Perhaps he or she has something you haven't read, or prose that lends itself to your ceremony. If you're interested in using scripture, ask a loved one for suggestions that may be unique or unusual for a wedding.

- Do you idolize your parents' marriage? Have they taught you the meaning of love and you cannot wait to embark on your own wedded path? Ask them what their wedding ceremony was like. Maybe there was a reading or ritual that would be a great addition to your own ceremony, and a nod to their lasting love.

- Fairy tales make for great ceremony readings. One of my favorite books growing up was a contemporary retelling of Rapunzel, and it was filled with gorgeous prose that would lend itself to any wedding. Whether you choose the original tales or modern versions, you're sure to find something special.

- Is Britney Spears' "You Drive Me Crazy" your all-time favorite guilty pleasure? Do you sing it to your fiancée constantly? Have a friend read a selection of lyrics. Some guests won't quite place it, others will appreciate the move, and you'll both share a mid-ceremony smile. (Mine is Mandy Moore's "Crush." I sing it to Sam all the time, and she can't help but smile because, ya know, Mandy Moore. It's irresistible.)

- Maybe a musical interlude is better than any reading or ritual. Have a niece who can play the ukulele? Get her up there.
- Have friends who are great writers? Or maybe a family member or just maybe you or your bride can pen something brilliant? You're allowed to include your own work or the work of a loved one in your ceremony. In fact, it would be a beautiful tribute.
- If you're not familiar with your culture's marriage traditions, do a little digging. You might find a really cool ritual your ancestors included in their wedding ceremonies.

When in doubt—read, read, read.

# In Memoriam

I'VE SHARED A FEW suggestions as to how we honored Sam's mother during our wedding. In fact, we honored many missing loved ones.

Anyone who has lost a loved one knows that life's milestones are forever bittersweet. It's okay to acknowledge loss and pay homage to the people that are present only in spirit, and in our hearts.

### Ideas for honoring lost loved ones

- Opening the ceremony with the lighting of a candle or even the releasing of a balloon is a poignant way to begin. Your officiant can say a few words about the ritual, and either bride can light the memory candle, or release the balloon. Having a candle glowing throughout our ceremony brought a comforting luminosity to the evening's events.
- Passing out programs to your guests? On the first page, include a list of those people you wish to remember.
- Have a loved one or perhaps your officiant read a poem or a prayer to keep them in everyone's thoughts throughout the ceremony.
- Keep an empty seat during your ceremony. You can put a photograph in it if you feel so inclined.
- Wear something that belonged to them.

- It's pretty common these days, but that didn't stop me from doing it at my own wedding. We had a table in the front of our reception that had a few uses. It held tall vases of gorgeous flowers. It was a place for gifts and cards, and we included wedding photos from our immediate family members. For one set of Sam's grandparents who were married in the 1940s, she found their wedding invitation and included it in its own frame.
- Quote them in a wedding speech, or have a member of your bridal party tell a funny or poignant story about them.

# First Look

T HE "FIRST LOOK" HAS become a modern day wedding tradition. It seems that couple's who don't have a first look—those couples who wait until the actual ceremony—are now the ones who are considered divergent. There are pros and cons to the first look and it helps to consider these before making a decision.

Sure, this idea that you don't see your bride until the wedding ceremony is a romantic one, but it's not always the most practical. The brides I've heard from are split. Many opt for a first look so they can get all their portrait photos finished before the wedding. Others want the romance of seeing each other when they're walking down the aisle. One couple even did it old school: the brides' families kept them from seeing each other from the night before their wedding right up until they joined hands for their wedding ceremony.

Sam and I chose not only to have a first look, but to spend most of our day together pre-ceremony. We had our loved ones surrounding us for only a couple of days. We did not want to waste this. We retreated to our cabin early afternoon to start getting ready. We had our hair and makeup done together before Sam disappeared to get dressed in a separate location. We hadn't seen each other's dresses and were determined to keep it that way until we were dressed and ready.

Our first look was on a floating dock outside of our cabin. I stood at the end of the dock facing the water and Sam joined me soon after. That moment is one of my favorites from our wedding. By the time Sam joined me on the dock my stress level had finally escalated—granted this was mostly due to the camera crews rushing to get me mic'd so my wedding could be on reality television, so this isn't really the "typical" wedding stress, but I digress—I was ready to see my bride. Each time I watch the video of our first look I recognize the elation on my face. Not only did my bride look stunning, but her mother's vintage headpiece (which she'd worn for her 1981 wedding) that Sam was so worried about looked exquisite with her gown. We are pretty bad at keeping secrets from each other, so our first look was the culmination of two brides choosing their bridal looks without once confiding in each other. Okay, okay, I told her I was wearing green. You can't really surprise a gal with a detail like that, lest she wear the wrong color palette. I knew that once I kissed her on that dock and our photographer began snapping photos, I could relax. We were now in this together.

The first look allows you the time to take photos without missing your wedding. That's the real draw of the first look. You get all those gorgeous portraits without feeling like you need to rush back to cocktail hour. You can remind each other to take deep breaths and relax before the ceremony. You can practice your kiss one final time. You can feel really beautiful because your bride keeps telling you how stunning you look… I can go on. If you're okay with doing away with the tradition of not seeing your bride before the ceremony, then I think a first look is for you. And of course, this doesn't have to be a big deal. Some brides don't have a first look because they don't actually separate. Like Alexis and Britt. They got ready together in their hotel suite and didn't spend a moment apart for their entire wedding day.

There are many ways in which a two-bride wedding deviates from a heterosexual wedding, but the ritual of getting ready is a place where we can easily blur the lines. Traditionally the bride is off with her bridesmaids primping for hours while the groom and his buddies are golfing or brunching or doing whatever it is that guys do.

When my wife and I are getting ready for an event I ask her if my makeup looks okay, I ask her which shoes to wear, she wants my opinion on her choice of skirt—we get the best of both worlds in that I get to have a spouse and a best friend and they're the same person. (Don't get me started on how much I love going to the spa with her and not having to separate by gender. The best.) So when it comes to getting ready for your wedding day you want that reassurance, but it's also nice to have the element of surprise.

If you're pretty adamant about not seeing each other until the ceremony it's not terribly hard to make that work with your timeline. You can extend your cocktail hour by thirty minutes to allot time for pictures. If your ceremony and reception are in separate locations you may have a window of time anyway. Sometimes ceremonies in churches, for instance, are held in the afternoon, and maybe the reception isn't until evening. This gives you plenty of time for photos.

I was really happy with how we did our first look and I would do it again. That's not to say there's nothing I would do differently. I did not leave enough time for pictures. I have no patience and didn't want to spend an hour traipsing the venue grounds taking photos. In retrospect, I wish I had. It's okay though, we got some amazing shots before and after the ceremony.

EXPERT TIP:

*Chelsea Mason, Photographer*

**What's your number one budget insider-savings tip?**

*At the end of the day, a good photographer is going to leave you with a higher bill. A budget friendly tip that all couples should think about when booking a photographer is to try and find someone who gives you the images digitally rather than makes you buy prints. Today more wedding images are viewed on social media than the walls of your home. It's a sad fact, but it's true. By hiring a photographer who is digital, you're free to print whatever size image you'd like.*

# Should One or Both of You Walk Down the Aisle?

I ASK EVERY SINGLE bride in every same-sex couple this question. It's a required question on the real wedding submission form for the website, 2Brides2Be.

I ask because its one of the most frequent questions I got during wedding planning: "who walks down the aisle first?" I was asked this question so often that I wrote about it in the *New York Observer* in summer 2012 as an attempt to lift the veil on this curious, mysterious, lesbian wedding. But during our initial wedding planning neither Sam nor myself actually knew how to answer this question—who did walk down the aisle first? How would we choose?

We both wanted to uphold the tradition of being escorted by our fathers, and neither one of us wanted to be waiting at the alter. Our solution revealed itself: we would have two aisles. We came from either side and met in the middle, making a V toward the deck where we had our ceremony. Of course, some guests complained that they wouldn't be able to see us both, but I shrugged and reminded them, "You have the entire ceremony to stare at us." Our two makeshift aisles—two wooded paths covered in wood chips—were perfect for us. I got to walk with my dad, which was important to me, but I also got to walk toward my bride as her own father escorted her to me. We all hugged and kissed on arrival and it truly felt like a meeting of two families. It established the familial warmth of our ceremony.

Jenna and Kayla were able to have an even better version of this "two aisle" feature. We were limited for space because our ceremony was in the woods, on a deck overlooking a lake. We had only so much space. Jenna and Kayla walked down to the beach off of a bluff, then had a huge sandy stage of their own. They created an upside down Y shaped aisle, so each walked with her parents toward the center where they met. From there the couple walked hand in hand down the leg of the Y toward their ceremony spot.

Friends, family, and wedding vendors alike, are going to say the wrong thing on occasion from the early planning sages through the last dance. I don't think any of us make it through unscathed, but we can decide how we react. You may hear some version of the following:

> *But you're so pretty, you should walk down the aisle.*

> *She's definitely the man in the relationship, so she should be waiting up there.*

*You're wearing a suit, why would you walk down the aisle?*

*She's so much more femme than you are, let her be the bride.*

Sound at all familiar?

First, try to laugh it off. Every one of these lines is ridiculous. I don't even have to explain why describing one bride as "prettier" than her future wife is a backhanded compliment, but the other lines are also false. Don't listen to them. I don't care if you have a buzz cut and you're wearing a custom bespoke suit to your wedding, if you want your father or mother or best friend to walk you down the aisle, then dammit, you are a bride, walk that aisle!

Brides Britt and Alexis were both escorted down the aisle by their moms. Britt, wearing a suit, went first. She explained, "Alexis was wearing a dress that seemed more worthy of a wait." Sounds like a nice compromise to me. Brides Katy and Claire decided to walk down the aisle together, in unity. Suzie and Lauren's guests were seated to form an infinity symbol and together the brides weaved through them. There are endless possibilities. Choose what feels natural for you.

There's also this: it's something of a legend in my mind now because I heard about it but have never seen it in action. If you're going a nontraditional route and want to begin the wedding with a little cocktail party, everyone can be hanging out drinking and chatting when suddenly, your officiant will stand in the middle of the crowd, then you and your bride will stand in front of him or her. Then your bridal party can surround you until all of the guests catch on that it's time, the ceremony is beginning. There is such a casual element to this, yet it feels so special. If you have done this or know someone who has, please, call me.

# Vows

SAM AND I KNEW that we would write our own vows. I guess I assumed that because ours wasn't a traditionally religious ceremony, there wasn't any particular wording we had to follow. Customizing our ceremony was a huge part of our wedding planning process, and writing our own vows fit in with this plan.

To be honest, we put it off. I feel like most people do, because, well, what do you say? There's the obvious pressure of feeling like this has to be both the most profound and romantic thing you've ever uttered, to impress not only your bride and, of course, the family and friends that surround you. And you don't want to make some silly little joke that, thirty years later, you're asking yourself, "What the hell was I talking about?"

I stressed about writing vows. I'm wordy. I write. Writing is how I communicate. Too many people were all, "Well we know your vows will be great." The pressure! The pressure! I did not know what to say to Sam that would speak both to our past, our present, and our future, that would acknowledge our imperfections but focus on the strength of our love for each other.

Our officiant, Elizabeth Phaire, gave us great guidance. She encouraged us to feel positive and empowered while speaking. I appreciated her advice, and for the most part, I followed it. I am sure that she didn't necessarily agree with every one of my choices in my vows, but I also reminded myself that we were writing our own vows for a reason.

Sam and I have never tried to come off as the perfect couple. We're a mess. We have a past leaden with stories of ways in which we hurt each other. Together we've experienced profound loss, trauma, and ya know what? We bicker. Like a lot. To stand there and make dazzling promises would have been an affront to our imperfect union, and so that's what I focused on: our imperfect union. I'm glad I did. Though much of our wedding ceremony is a blacked-out haze (I swear this happens—out of body experience), I do remember willing myself to be wholly present when we spoke our vows. These were our words, ours only, and we were stating them with witnesses (a lot of them) and sincerity.

A few weeks before our wedding, when I was still panicking about what to write, Sam's friend Kate gave us a great piece of advice. She told us to choose a mood for our vows, a common thread that would connect our focus. Are you both quoting poets? Are you telling a story? Are you keeping things light, or are you softly weeping a list of promises? It's good to have an answer to this and be able to share it with your bride-to-be. I think this was excellent advice.

Ever been to a wedding and the vows go something like this?

> *Spouse #1: Tearful, romantic, flowery, dramatic.*

> *Spouse #2: Joke, joke, quote about love, joke.*

I'm not choosing a side here. Funny vows are awesome. Tearful vows are awesome. But Kate was right, it's best if both brides are coming from a similar place when they speak. This will maintain a tone for your ceremony and have you staring into each other's eyes while you're both thinking: *I fucking love you*, and, *we got this.*

Sam and I said we would do this and then kind-of-sort-of tried and then kinda stopped talking to each other about it. Still, our vows were similar in tone.

Mine began with this:

> *Though I knew I loved you early on, I could never be sure specifically why. Maybe it was because I never imagined that there was a person on this earth who could perceive me so completely. Or maybe it was because whenever I was with you I felt the most captivating fusion of comfort, fever, and bliss. Whatever it was, it stuck.*

Sam's began with this:

> *I feel like my life began when I met you. You've taught me so much about myself, sometimes it's unbelievable to think of who*

*I was before you. Because of your patience and your love I've become a reliable, caring, and unselfish person that loves you with all of my heart. Falling in love with you wasn't just a temporary madness. It was something that never subsided.*

Mine included this:

*I may never be the superlative wife. I'm always going to be messy, and always going to be stubborn, but I am always going to be faithful to our marriage, our family, and our dreams. Our union may not be perfect, but it will be raucous and unruly and perfectly us.*

Sam's included this:

*I want you to know that I believe in you, the person you will grow to be, and the couple that we will be together. With my whole heart, I take you as my wife, allowing and accepting your faults and strengths, as you do mine. I promise to be faithful and supportive and to always make our family's love and happiness my priority.*

Sam got choked up during her vows. I remind her of this on a daily basis, especially if I'm annoying her more than usual. She'll say something like, "You're so aggravating I think I hate you."

"Oh yeah?" I'll say. "Then why did you cry during your vows?" Without pausing for her to answer I always say, "You're so obsessed with me."

It's okay to feel inspired by vows you've heard at other weddings. My friend said to her almost-husband during their ceremony, "I vow in this life to find you in the next." My knees buckled at her beautiful words. What a glorious line. And she meant it. Other friends have mentioned ways in which their spouse has made them a better person, whether they're more positive or have a better sense of humor. Are you a die-hard sports fan? You can mention that you love her more than your number-one team. Your vows are your chance to say a few words to each other with loved ones bearing witness, so give them the attention they deserve, but do not fall into a pit of anxiety over what to say.

EXPERT TIP:

*Elizabeth Phaire, Master Life-Cycle Celebrant® and Interfaith Minister:*

**What's the biggest mistake you see brides making?**

*Taking care of all other wedding details and hiring their officiant last. Especially if the couple wants a personalized ceremony, it's hard to find the right officiant if they're rushing last minute, and most are already booked by then. After you book your venue research your officiant next, to allow time to find the right person for you, and there's a better chance they will be available for your date.*

*Helpful prompts*

- **You can take the *common thread* suggestion and choose a topic**. Maybe you want your vows to be about unity or compromise. Maybe you want to focus on your journey as a couple, or your dreams for your future.

- **Set the tone.** Vows can be poignant with a little humor on the side, but make sure you're both on the same page as to how funny or solemn your words should be.

- **Make lists.** Each of you can write down your ten favorite things about each other. Or write down ten common goals for the years ahead. Lists help get your brain working.

- **Set a word count.** If your bride's vows go on for ten minutes and yours for two, there's a clear imbalance. Maybe you'll both shoot for five hundred to eight hundred words, which will give you a similar length.
- **Stories have a beginning, middle, and end.** Your vows can, too. Maybe you both begin your vows talking about a memory from early in your relationship, then what marriage means to you, and finish with your intentions for a future together.
- Maybe you don't want to write your own vows but you don't want to follow the usual "in sickness and in health." Go ahead and **use someone else's words**. You can take turns reciting stanzas from a favorite poem, or each share a meaningful quote that embodies your feelings

When you're saying these vows—project! Your guests want to hear you, that's why they're present.

# The Pronouncement

Y ou, your fiancée, and your officiant will decide together how you would like to be addressed when you're officially a married couple. This decision might seem insignificant, but my wife and I went back and forth about how we wanted to be presented. Perhaps you want to be called by your new name, or maybe you prefer a wish for your future. Here are some ideas to get you started:

- I present Mrs. And Mrs. Smith
- I now pronounce you wife and wife
- I now pronounce you joined in love, life, and marriage
- You are officially married and I invite you both to kiss your bride
- You are now married in the state of Massachusetts
- In front of your family and friends, it is my honor to welcome you into your marriage
- Ladies and gentlemen, the newlyweds!

I loved the idea of being pronounced wife and wife. That is what I feel that we are, and the words felt right for the moment. Go ahead and ask your officiant to speak words that feel authentic to you as a couple.

# The Kiss

I KNOW THE WEDDING kiss is something all couples think about, but let's be honest here, two women kissing in front of their family and friends for possibly the first time ever? That's pressure.

Something I find funny is that long before Sam and I talked about what kind of wedding we would have, or even when we would get married, we practiced *the kiss*. She'd always initiate, by pulling me close and saying, "How you gonna kiss me at our wedding?" And inevitably we would drop what we were doing to practice the perfect smooch. *Can't be too sexy*, we'd say. "No tongue," Sam would reprimand. *But can't be too platonic, either*, we'd agree. I'd make Sam perch onto the little step-stool we use to reach our sheets and towels in the top of our closets. I'd say, "You'll have to be wearing high heels and I'll wear flats." I assumed the stool created the right height ratio. We'd fumble with our hands. "No, put yours on my hip." I'd tell her as I rested my hand in the crook of her neck. By the time we were actually engaged and in the throes of wedding planning, we got pretty serious about this kiss.

"Let's film it," I told Sam one day while we were folding laundry. Like a pitcher reviewing footage, I thought we could literally zoom in on our performance and see what needed work.

You guys. I know this is crazy. I have no memories—aside from a peck—of kissing Sam in front of my extended family before our wedding. I wanted everyone to watch this kiss and weep. I wanted them to stand and demand, "Marriage equality must be the law of the land!" (It wasn't yet in 2013.) And I wanted all the aunts and uncles, second cousins, and bosses past to get used to this idea of wife and wife. This is a ridiculous notion, to think that a kiss can change so much, but iconic kisses have been known to linger throughout history. Images that come to mind include *Bruderkiss* on the Berlin Wall, and the American World War II soldier smooching a nurse in Times Square upon his return from war. Kisses matter. That's why marriage vows are sealed with them.

What happened on our wedding day was exactly what you'd expect. We were lost in the moment. I tell my friends not to be nervous for their wedding ceremony, that it won't matter because they're simply going to black out. I'm only half kidding. The moment takes you and you don't think, you just react. You're standing there with your beloved experiencing all of these rituals; vows and rings, handfastings or blessings, and you're just waiting to kiss her. So by the time you get to lay one on her, what's revealed is pure, unfiltered love. Our kiss, by the way, went great. Sam had her hand on my face and I had my hand on her waist and we kissed and then kissed some more. Everyone was hooting and hollering and the moment was everything I had no idea it could be.

I asked a few other women with wives how their wedding kisses went. KD spent most of her ceremony fidgeting, fearing the kiss would turn out too sultry, or too chaste. In the end, she says, it was great. She smiled through the kiss, making it neither sultry nor chaste but giggly instead. Lauren and her bride-to-be practiced their kiss again and again, knowing a peck simply wouldn't cut it, and Katrina describes hers, simply, as *awkward.com*. Laura reports that she was "totally nervous," that all she could think about were her in-laws watching her kiss their daughter. Kolby avoided nerves altogether. She and her bride eloped, kissed a whole bunch of times, then giggled in excitement.

Guess what—all the brides survived it. And looking back, most agree it was one of the best parts of their wedding day. So practice if you want. Or go off script and wing it. My only advice is to kiss her. Kiss her long and kiss her good.

# Marriage License and Name Change

THESE ARE TWO THINGS that need to be on your radar as you plan your wedding, unless you don't intend to be legally married.

If you're not changing your names, then you need only a marriage license. A simple online search will tell you how to obtain a marriage license from your county clerk. If you're changing your name or names, however, there might be more to it.

### So. How do you decide?

Before our marriage, I was a Semon (pronounced "see-min") and my wife Sam was a Goettlich (pronounced "get-lick"). Though it doesn't produce the same immediate lascivious reactions as Semon, when the two are paired, like a great steak and a full-bodied Cabernet, the results are exquisite. How did two women with such tenacious last names end up together? A cruel consequence of fate, our love stopped me from achieving my childhood dream of marrying into a classic last name.

In our early courtship we didn't worry about a last name. But then came wedding planning, and as members of a community historically unrecognized in marriage, we consider it important that we share the same last name and pass it down to our children. Many of our same-sex friends chose whichever name worked best. Some are attached to their own names, some not so much. Some of them consider male heirs to the family name; others consider their names in relation to their careers. Some are open to hyphenating. For same-sex couples who plan to keep one of their names, the name-change process in the state of New York is identical to that of straight couples.

Neither Sam nor myself was keen to take the other's name, and hyphenating was not an option. Our friends had a blast conjuring suggestions like Semonlich and Goetsemon. "Our poor future children," I lamented. "Our poor unborn babies," Sam replied. We imagined our future child on his first day of school, hair combed into the appropriate style, homemade lunch of roasted veggie quinoa and baby-arugula-with-pear-and-goat-cheese salad tucked into his superhero lunch box, looking around the cafeteria for a friend. At each table he would stop to sit, only to be met with sneers. "Can't sit here, Goettlich-Semon. Why don't you go home and sit with your mommies?!" It was clear that we needed a new name altogether.

Negotiations began. We considered hyphenating our moms' maiden names. We considered names passed down through our families, and finally we decided to do something that many other couples, both straight and gay, have done before us: we took Sam's middle name as our last name. That decision turned out to be the easy part.

Next we needed to find out how to change our names. The tedious process had nothing at all to do with gay marriage. Had either one of us chosen to take the other's last name, the process would have been easy. The marriage license would have allowed either spouse to take the surname of the other. That being said, we certainly confused some of the employees downtown who couldn't quite figure out why two women were simultaneously changing their surnames to Abby, so it sounds like what we've done is a little out of the ordinary.

We each had to petition the court for a name change. I filed out paperwork online, and the petition involved a sixty-five dollar fee for each of us. We brought our completed copies down to civil court along with birth certificates and exact change for the various undisclosed fees. (For instance: because I was born in New York they kept my birth certificate and I had to pay for a copy. Sam was born in New Jersey so they simply photocopied hers. No idea what the logic is here.)

The following week we returned to court to see the judge. If your experience is anything like ours, you will enter a large, windowless room and cautiously approach the court officer, who has no patience for your confusion. He'll swipe the papers from your hand and tell you to sit down, and without any prompting, he will let you know, "You're gonna be here awhile." You will sit silently and fearfully. A judge will enter, but you will not talk to him. Then some guy will call your name, and ask you some questions. Then you sit back down and wait another forty minutes, when a woman will start handing out your petitions as the judge reminds you to read your documents thoroughly, because even if they got it wrong, once you leave here, this is your new, permanent name. They tell you which newspaper you're required to publish with. Our judge chose the *Irish Echo*, so when I called a day later, I spoke to a lovely Irish lass named Mary, who charged me seventy dollars for two name-change publications, which were published the following week. Upon publication we received an affidavit, which we took back to court where we finalized the paperwork and bought certified copies of our name-change documents. It was a snap!

From there the process is similar to the usual name change, which can be completed on the marriage license. Our next stops were the social security office and the DMV. These are the parts of getting married that are the opposite of a good time. My advice is to get on top of this stuff early.

These tedious details are not the ones you want to be rushing through at the last minute, so don't wait until the day before your wedding. Marriage licenses do expire, however, so don't go too early either. My advice if you're petitioning the court for a name change? Do it sooner rather than later.

Every couple, straight or gay, has their own view on this name change. It's worth a discussion early on in marriage planning, just to get on the same page and have time to get used to the idea of a new name.

# PART FIVE

## *The Celebration*

THE BEST RESULT OF the stress and the spending of wedding planning is certainly the celebrating. There are more ways than you can even imagine to celebrate your wedding, whether you're steadfast in following tradition or you're forging your own path. There are opportunities in the months leading up to your wedding day to enjoy the support of loved ones, so you should take advantage.

When it comes to *the big day*, I tend to think that Sam and I skipped many wedding traditions, but to be honest, there are a whole lot of them. No couple can possibly do everything, lest their wedding zooms by in a flurry of bouquet tosses and cake-cutting, first dances and speeches. Our relationship, our family, and our cultural traditions are an easy way to make some of these choices. The truth is, Sam and I had so many traditional elements in our wedding, some were spiritual, others cultural, and some, of course, just plain fun.

Even in my single days I skipped the bouquet toss. I was never into moments on the dance floor that disrupted the natural rhythm of guests having fun. One minute everyone's breaking it down and spilling prosecco, the next the guests are asked to leave so a chosen group can occupy the dance floor. Some brides adore this. Some guests are heartbroken if you don't throw the bouquet, but the point is, at your wedding, you get to do only the elements that feel right for you. The celebration is the part where you must let go and enjoy, because this is it. Don't miss it.

## EXPERT TIP:

Stephanie Karvellas-Baynton, Owner & Venue Coordinator at Cedar Lakes Estate

**Anything you try to steer couples away from?**

*Making traditions that mean nothing to them a part of their wedding because they think they have to. For instance, if you don't want to cut the cake, don't waste hundreds of dollars on a cake! Get a fun dessert that represents you as a couple and make your own tradition. We had a bride and groom sip a giant root beer float because they met at a Stewart's.*

# Make it Your Own

BY NOW I'M SURE you have plenty of inspiration from stories I've shared, as well as your own tremendous ideas on how to make your wedding all about you and your bride. But let's face it, industry experts know best, so I turned to some trusted insiders for the scoop on how to kick a two-bride wedding up a notch.

### How can a couple put their twist on a classic wedding element?

**Breck Hofstedder of Sesame Letterpress** says she loves custom envelope liners. Couples can have a more traditional invitation design, but then do something more expressive and unexpected for the envelope liner. It can be a bright color or pattern or maybe a map of the wedding location or where you met. "This is a nice place to add some fun but not water down the formality of the design too much."

**DJ Keelez** says that if you want to incorporate a classical music feel without the "classical music feel," check out groups like Vitamin String Quartet or 2Cellos. They take popular songs and perform them with classical instruments. Very cool.

**Elizabeth Phaire, Master Life-Cycle Celebrant® and Interfaith Minister,** explains that classic rituals usually incorporate one or more of the four elements: earth, air, fire, water. You can take the universal symbolism of an element and weave it with the personal significance it holds for you as a couple.

"One example might be a modern interpretation of the Jewish Seven Blessings, which are spoken over a Kiddush Cup filled with wine (or grape juice or other beverage). Grape juice and wine are considered the 'fruit of the vine' because grapes come from the earth, which represents stability and abundance. The blessings can incorporate this symbolism and be written especially for the couple, or use a pre-written modern version. Alternatively, the couple can choose seven of their family and friends to each write a blessing that they would read over the Kiddush Cup, which the couple then drinks from. It becomes a poignant moment as the couple is blessed by their closest loved ones."

**Hair Stylist Jill Hammelman** loves when a bride incorporates a personal item from the wedding day of a loved one who has passed, whether it be the headpiece their mother wore or tying a grandmother's wedding ring into the bouquet.

**Owner and Chef Lisa Karvellas of Cedar Lakes Estate** thinks it's important to put your personality into your wedding food. "The best time to do that is during cocktail hour." If you have a favorite restaurant, ask them and your caterer if they could contribute in some way. One of Lisa's couples grew up on the Lower East Side of Manhattan and went to Katz's deli their whole lives. Lisa and her staff picked up their famous pastrami and made mini versions of their pastrami reuben "sliders" to pass during the cocktail hour. It made the experience even more personal and special.

**Meg Nobile, Florist and Designer at That Time Events,** says that letting your personalities shine through is where the twists come in. "I had a couple who met over a cup of tea. For the cocktail hour we put all the flowers in vintage tea tins. It was a design element that was special to them and something unique and different for their guests to enjoy."

**Makeup Artist Sharon Becker** loves when clients get creative with their makeup. "Many clients love a Hollywood winged liner, and I suggest updating that with a navy or deep violet gel liner." She also says that while pop lips are very popular, clients can wear the trend without having it wear them by using a dash of bright lipstick, blotting, and finishing with non-shiny lip balm to make a modern stained lip.

**Stephanie Karvellas-Baynton, Owner and Venue Coordinator at Cedar Lakes Estate,** urges couples to think about what experiences have shaped their relationship. "Is it through food, travel, work, drinks, etc.? If you focus on creating an experience for your guests that represents you then your wedding will stand out." Some examples:

- Bride and bride exited their wedding ceremony to an acoustic version of "I Kissed a Girl."
- Bride was obsessed with French fries—passed cups of French fries at the after-party, all her friends loved it!
- Couple met in New Orleans—did a second line dance and passed out umbrellas and beads to everyone at their wedding reception!
- Couple got engaged in Nantucket—displayed a vintage canoe filled with their favorite Nantucket brewer's beers at their cocktail hour.
- Groom was always worrying about what him and his groomsman would do while the girls got hair and makeup done, so the bride surprised him with a pop up barber shop with hot shaves for all the guys!

### Can you share a great suggestion specifically for a two-bride wedding?

**Breck Hofstedder of Sesame Letterpress** loves a cleverly worded response card or information card.

**DJ Keelez** recommends putting a fun spin on a traditional element like the bouquet or garter toss. Instead of tossing a bouquet, both brides can toss a football or a stuffed animal that matches their individual personalities. Instead of pulling the garter out from under the dress you can pull out a tool belt or a Kelly Clarkson CD. Anything that you know will get a smile or laugh from your guests. It lightens the mood and makes for a fantastic night.

**Elizabeth Phaire, Master Life-Cycle Celebrant®
and Interfaith Minister,** believes that two brides are
better than one because "between the three of us it's
triple creativity." What would be spectacular really
depends on the couple's tastes, their venue, and the
overall vision for the ceremony. "That's the beauty
of working of working with a Life-Cycle Celebrant®;
we explore ideas and discover what would be
spectacular for you as a unique couple."

**Hair Stylist Jill Hammelman** loves brides who
wait until the first look to see each other's dresses.
"Get your bridal trials together and even get ready
together on your wedding day, but keep your dresses
a secret and have a beautiful first-look moment."

**Owner and Chef Lisa Karvellas of Cedar Lakes
Estate** suggests menu ideas based on her favorite
weddings. "The Abby wedding really wrote the
book on lesbian weddings at Cedar Lakes Estate...
they designed their menus with all of their favorite
foods in mind. This included a seasonal tomato
and burrata salad, mini taco salad, and New York
favorites like miniature hot dogs and knishes. The
s'mores were a nod to the night they got engaged,
and we even made a gingerbread-smashed ice cream
that one of the brides fell in love with during a trip
to Seattle."

**Meg Nobile, Florist and Designer at That Time
Events,** says that she works the language of flowers
into all of her arrangements. "It would be lovely for

each bride to design their future wife's bouquet and surprise them at their first look, and talk about what they chose in their vows."

For example, a bouquet filled with Austrian rose, white ivy, red dahlia, cedar, and Virginian creeper can translate to: "I am filled with joy, for you are all that is lovely and rare. I live for you and will cling to you in both sunshine and shade."

**Stephanie Karvellas-Baynton, Owner and Venue Coordinator at Cedar Lakes Estate,** says, "Trash your wedding gowns by using our double zip line that will land you straight into the lake!"

*I love these suggestions, and here's a few more of my own:*

- For your rehearsal dinner serve wines that have meaning to you as a couple. Did you explore Napa for your first anniversary together? Serve a Cabernet you fell in love with in that region. Maybe you spend your summers hanging at the wineries on Long Island, choose a sauvignon blanc from one of your favorites. Guests will always appreciate the story behind what they're experiencing at your wedding.
- Serve your favorite spirits as passed shots during the reception. Many couples steer away from having bartenders pour shots at their wedding, and you might be the same. During the last hour of the party, however, it's time to let loose.

Have hers and hers shots passed around the dance floor.

- Wrap your bouquets in each other's dress material.
- Lend each other jewelry for your "something borrowed."
- Have a friend or sibling act as the night's master of ceremonies. My brother took this job at my wedding and it was so much fun having special moments like dances or speeches introduced with a dose of humor.

# Rehearsal Dinner

REHEARSAL DINNERS USED TO be just that, rehearsals followed by dinner for bridal parties and immediate family. This tradition has transformed and many couples are now focusing on incorporating most or all of their wedding guests into the events for the night before the wedding. If everyone's in town, why not kick-off the wedding weekend as a group? This is especially great because by the time you say your vows the next day, many of your guests that arrived as strangers will now be friends, and you'll feel like you've spent time with everyone, which will help keep you from spreading yourself thin on your wedding day. No bride wants to spend her entire wedding catching up with her dad's colleagues or second cousin once removed.

I've heard of brides planning rehearsal dinners two days before their wedding so they can "get wasted" and still be fresh for their wedding day. As a girl who loves to rage, even I think this is overkill, and often the sign of a bride who is perhaps a little immature. Still, there are other reasons for rehearsal dinners being a day or so prior to the wedding, and whatever your reason, you need to do what you have to do so that you're well rested for your wedding day.

Rehearsal dinners are also a great time for speeches, especially if you don't want to spend an entire hour of your wedding reception listening to toasts—this is not what I paid my band for.

Sam and I kept our wedding night speeches to the classics: fathers and maid of honor/best man. We wanted, however, to open the floor to friends and family who wanted to speak and Friday night was the perfect time. At a friend's rehearsal night a year prior she invited us to say a few words and not only did I feel honored to speak on behalf of my friend, but I think she and her husband-to-be really enjoyed all the toasts. I knew this would be great fun.

If you need plans in place to keep everyone from drinking too much, great ideas include bowling, shuffleboard, or other group activities. We had a beautiful evening and a giant lawn on a lake, so we showed a movie on a large screen while guests relaxed on blankets and snacked on popcorn. It's also good to remember that you can only be responsible for yourself. At friend's rehearsal dinners I tend to drink Chardonnay like every sip is my last. There's just so much excitement when everyone's finally together and "it's really happening!" If you don't want to provide alcohol for everyone all night, no worries, that's not your job, but if all of your college friends decide to hit the hotel bar and stay there until four in the morning, well, that's on them. You just get your butt to bed.

If your budget doesn't allow you to include anyone who isn't immediate family, invite guests to "welcome drinks" and pick up some of the tab, or simply ask guests to meet at a bar to enjoy a drink with the brides before their big day. Most business owners will want to help you out, because once most of your guests arrive they're likely to stay the evening. So speak to a manager about securing a few bottles of prosecco for a toast with your loved ones, then you're free to slip out for a good night's rest.

I recommend taking something to sleep.

Three tried and tested and really good tips for the night before your wedding:

**Don't drink too much.**
**Slip out early.**
**Get some sleep.**

EXPERT TIP:

*Lisa Karvellas, Owner and Chef at Cedar Lakes Estate*

**What's the biggest mistake you see
brides making?**

*Making huge menu sacrifices for one or two guests. If you only get three entrée choices, don't feel like at least one of them needs to be a gluten-free, dairy-free, soy-free, vegan option. Really look through your guest list and pinpoint how many people have real dietary restrictions. I find that in most cases, it really is only a handful, so ask your caterer if they could provide a couple of special meals for those people instead of making it a part of the core menu for all guests.*

### Rehearsal dinner 101

#### So, who's paying?

- Once you have an established budget you'll know if your entire guest list can attend or if you're just looking at immediate family and bridal parties. Did Uncle Jim and Aunt Barbara pay for the rehearsal dinner? Raise a glass in their honor. If your parents split the cost, then thank them, too. Anyone who helped you out deserves a shout-out tonight.

#### Do you actually need to rehearse?

- These days rehearsal dinners are often just the kick-off to the wedding weekend. Sometimes there is not actually a rehearsal. Maybe this is because the venue is unavailable, or your officiant is unavailable. If this is the case and you have a wedding party and procession, then it's important to gather everyone together and go over the plan. My sister-in-law did not have access to her venue so we all met up in the back of the rehearsal dinner venue for twenty minutes so we could go over the plan for the next day. Once we all knew what order to walk in and who we would be walking with we felt much better about the whole thing. Another friend, married in New Orleans, did not have access to her venue either. Rather than worry about it the night before, she built an extra twenty minutes into her wedding day so that we could go through the processional once before guests arrived. Everything went off without a hitch.

### What are your responsibilities to your guests?

- The rehearsal dinner is an excellent chance to spend time with older relatives or guests you may not want to be sitting with while all of your favorite songs are playing the next night. However you choose to budget your time, do make sure you get a chance to share pleasantries with everyone in attendance.

### Should you try to see everyone?

- Here's the thing: chances are that most of your guests will be in town the night before your wedding. So again, even if your budget won't allow you to pay for dinner and drinks for everyone, the spirit of merriment will be contagious, so it's not a bad idea to choose a local bar and let everyone know what time to meet up. Have a hometown minor league baseball team you love? Tell everyone to get tickets and enjoy a night outside. Having a destination wedding? Nothing beats a pool party.

### What kind of venue makes a great rehearsal dinner?

- If you're having a rehearsal, then a restaurant near your church, for instance, is a best bet. You don't want your guests doing too much driving, and you won't want to, either. Maybe there's a local restaurant that serves family-style Italian. That's perfect. Sam and I chose an open-air BBQ with a bluegrass playlist. Because of the laid-back vibe, many guests still tell me that was their favorite part of the entire weekend. Don't get too crazy about the rehearsal dinner. I've heard so many stories of brides getting in knock-down drag-outs with their in-laws who have agreed to pay for the rehearsal dinner but don't want to drop ten grand inviting a hundred people to dinner. Find a compromise or forfeit other people's money.

---

**EXPERT TIP:**

*Sharon Becker, Makeup Artist*

**Anything you steer couples away from?**

*Trust your artist when she makes a timeline for you. She does this every day and knows the way to get the whole party done on time, with smiles and laughs, in a relaxed and seamless manner.*

# Wedding Day

IF YOU'RE WAKING UP the morning of your wedding—congrats! You slept! That's a key element of your wedding day (hence my advice to fight the urge to party too hard the night before).

If you've considered your emotional well-being, then I am hopeful you have a nice, calm morning planned. There's nothing better than enjoying a cup of tea or coffee lazily smirking at your bride-to-be thinking, *It's here. We're getting married. It's happening.* Enjoying the entire day is key, which is why I've been sharing my own experiences and those of other brides in the previous pages. You've done all the planning. Now it's time to (try to) relax.

If you don't have a free second during the day because it's time for hair and makeup, last minute this and that, before your better-start-on-time ceremony, then that's okay, too. No matter what this day has in store for you, go ahead and kick it off with the following:

**If you're with your bride-to-be**: Take her hands in yours. Look her in the eyes. Take deep breaths. Smile. Giggle. Remind yourselves why you're here. This day is going to fly by so make a vow before *the* vow to be present. It's too late to worry, so roll with the punches and let yourself enjoy this.

**If you're not with your bride-to-be**: Send her a romantic text. Tell her you love her, that this is the day you've waited for your entire life, and that you're determined to be present for its entirety. Suggest she does the same. Turn to your bridesmaids, or family—whoever is surrounding you right now—and give them a squeeze. Let out a squeal. Now, take a deep breath. Take another. It's too late to worry, so roll with the punches and let yourself enjoy this.

Now that you've done your morning deep breathing, it's time to get this day started.

### *If you ignore all of my advice on your wedding day, do not ignore this: EAT*

You won't want to eat. You won't even feel hungry. And if you're like me, this will be a new and unusual feeling. Unless you're the kinda gal who can survive on a handful of almonds once in a while (I don't know anyone who can) then carve some time out of your day and eat. People will bring you food, I promise. All you have to do is chew and swallow.

Sam and I planned our wedding obsessively. Our timeline for the weekend was perfect. We had gone over it with the entire staff. Everyone knew what to do and where to be and how this was all going down. We planned obsessively so that the moment our guests began to arrive on Friday evening we could let go. That was it. We'd done all we needed to do and we were simply not going to worry any more. It was time to let go and be present for all that was about to go down.

I didn't have a wedding party and with a ceremony starting at six o'clock, I did not want to waste my wedding day. You have a whole group of your favorite people in the same place to celebrate with you and you're going to sit in a hotel room getting your hair curled all day? Don't do it.

Because I had a wedding at a summer-camp-turned-wedding-venue, Sam and I wanted to utilize the space and enjoy the weather during these last days of summer. Our wedding day began with breakfast for all guests staying on the grounds, and then we donned our kegs and kickball T-shirts. My loyal guests grabbed *Team Semon* tees, and Sam's grabbed *Team Goettlich* tees. Those of us in the game met on the baseball diamond, where naturally, we had a keg in the dugout. We spent the rest of the morning screaming and running around through a rousing kickball game. Sam's team won, though there have been whispers of cheating… She was presented with a giant trophy as they hoisted her up and ran her around the field. For this reason alone I'm glad we had our photographer on site. We also had lake activities for guests who weren't team players. These guests went zip lining into the lake and bruised their bodies on the blob. We kickball players joined them in the lake before Sam and I snapped a few photos in our kickball gear and disappeared into our cabin for the remainder of the afternoon.

As everyone else swam and drank and enjoyed lunch by the pool, we began our beautification process with my sister, our sister-in-law, and our mother and godmother. Girlfriends stopped by over the course of the next couple of hours for a champagne toast and some updates on how much drinking was going on outside. Our amazing venue owners showed up with a picnic and, yes, we ate.

As far as I was concerned, the first half of the day was a total success.

---

### EXPERT TIP:

*Jill Hammelman, Hair Design*

**What's the most important detail brides should look for when choosing a hair stylist?**

*Find a stylist who gets you. It's very important your stylist understands you, your style, and what you want. Many brides are not exactly sure what they want on their big day, in fact more more than half of my brides actually change their mind on the day of. So most importantly, make sure your stylist will listen to you and understands your style.*

---

I've been in friend's weddings and had enjoyable days that were less erratic and more wedding-focused. For a friend's Long Island wedding we spent the day at her parents' house listening to music, getting our hair and makeup done, and drinking champagne. For another friend's wedding down south we went running, hit up the bride's favorite bakery, and laid out by the pool before meeting in her suite to get ready together. There are many ways to enjoy your wedding day and it's only a matter of deciding who you want to spend it with and planning according to your desires.

I stayed with my bride until our hair and makeup was complete and it was time to get dressed. At that time she headed to a neighboring cabin while I stayed put. We reconvened on a dock some time later for our "first look."

# How Should You Feel?

I HAVE NO IDEA what's considered normal for a wedding day. Some people feel nervous, others can't stop crying because they're so damn happy and emotional. For as long as I can remember I've been a step behind my emotions. I won't cry during goodbyes. In fact I'll probably look totally aloof, but give me a day or two and then, wow, waterworks. I always need some time to process. So on my wedding day I don't remember feeling overwhelmed by the weight of the occasion. I just remember being happy. I was surrounded by everyone I love, for the first and probably last time in my life, and they were all there in support of my marriage. There was no one else in the world I'd rather be marrying that day. It was just this constant feeling of "holy shit this is awesome."

Some brides use their wedding day to just totally freak out. I worried I might be one of those people. I used to stress about any gathering I was hosting. I could be throwing a party at my apartment with a guest list of fifteen people and suddenly I would have zero patience for Sam, who could do nothing right. My hair would look terrible, I'd be bordering on tears, and, really, all I had to do was put the baked brie in the oven and buy some ice. Luckily all of my freak-outs came in the days before the wedding, so that on the big day I was feeling pretty calm. Sure, there will be high-stress moments. Things will go wrong.

Let me repeat this: *Things will go wrong.*

This is an absolute guarantee. It's okay though, for two reasons: 1) Whatever goes wrong will likely be minute details. 2) Nobody will notice.

I swear, no one will notice if your florist forgot the vases of baby's breath in the women's bathroom. A year after your wedding you won't remember either. You'll know there were a few hiccups but you won't be able to recall what, exactly, they were. So don't let stupid crap ruin your day. There will be plenty of opportunities in the future to sulk or throw a tantrum. Whatever you get the day of your wedding, go with it. Enjoy it.

And don't worry that you're not "emotional enough." You're fine. The only thing you need to be is in the moment, making the very best of the rain or wind or sunshine. Be your best self and enjoy this special day.

# What to Wear?

**N**OW IS A GOOD time to be unique, especially when it comes to weddings. From couture ball gowns to custom bespoke suits, there is no shortage of design possibilities in bridal fashion. If you can dream it up you can wear it for your wedding, whether your budget is $100 or $10,000.

So why read on? What is there to know? It's lovely when I'm at a wedding and the groom's look is reflective of what his bride is wearing. Be it black tie and tails with beaded gowns, or a bride in ethereal antique white and a groom in suspenders, it looks so effortless. So can two brides look just as complementary? You can. But it might take some finesse.

Are you going gown and your bride is going jumpsuit? Lucky you, this might be easy. Are you and your bride both looking for a silk taffeta drop waist and sweetheart neckline? Okay, you can rock the same dress if it feels right, but you might want to make some tweaks to ensure that you both look your best and that, most importantly, you look smashing together.

You must also keep this in mind: don't wear something that's not you. If you haven't worn a dress since your First Communion, why start now? Says bride Claire about the attempts to outfit herself and her fiancée, "This is what we struggled with the most. It nearly made us call the whole thing off!" Her fiancée tried on dresses but nothing felt right, and the brides finally concluded that they wanted to feel comfortable. Once they let go of unrealistic style expectations, they were able to find suits that looked great and made them feel good.

EXPERT TIP:

*Daniel Friedman, Bindle and Keep Bespoke Suitmaker*

**Anything you steer couples away from?**

*Avoid beige and super light pink shirts. Most of your guests will be wearing white and your off-white shirt will look less crisp. Any shirt that that looks like it was washed with a red towel or matches the cream hue of your old white underwear is not a good color choice for your wedding. If you want to match the crème tint of the wedding dress it's always better to do it with accents, i.e. the pocket square and bowtie. So many of our clients place way too much emphasis on being matchy-matchy and it's not necessary. Everyone in the wedding will know it's your day, whether the two of you color coordinate or not. It's probably important to also note it is not necessary to include your wedding colors in your suit attire. Save the color combos for tablecloths and invitations! Your guests won't, for the life of them, notice, but they'll certainly remember your funny loden-green tie overwhelming every wedding picture.*

### *There are a few kinds of women*

There's the woman who has always known exactly what she will wear to her wedding.

There's the woman that's pretty particular but swears she'll stay open-minded.

There's the woman who doesn't really know what to wear.

And there's the woman who not only has no idea what to wear, she dreads the entire process.

I was the second type. My wife was the last.

"I'm wearing green. I've always known it," I told her. "I don't know what I'm wearing," she sighed, "but it'll probably be something messy." It wasn't much. But it was a start.

Are you dreaming of green? How about purple? Blue? As much as I love a surprise, you might think about telling your bride-to-be. Case-in-point? My wife tried on a black and pink Vera Wang that was quickly a frontrunner for her, but when she pictured an emerald grown next to it, she realized we would look terribly mismatched, and I'd already called dibs on green.

Do not be afraid to go out of your comfort zone, at least in the beginning. I knew I would be having my dress made, but that meant I needed to go try on wedding gowns so I knew what silhouette I was after.

What did I have in mind? Lace, very little structure, probably a sheath. My friend Lauren and I had a lunch date on a rainy afternoon in Soho then walked over to the Nicole Miller showroom. I've always loved her gowns. They're approachable, but they still make a woman look feminine and effortlessly beautiful. I pulled dresses in my chosen silhouette and it quickly became clear—this wasn't working for me. I willed myself not to freak out about how bad I looked. Lauren pulled a silk taffeta sweetheart with a drop-waist from the rack. "I would wear this," she said. "It's beautiful." I scoffed. "That's not me. I'm not into strapless, and it's a little—" I motioned *big, poufy, dramatic* with my hands. "Shut up," she told me. "Just try it on." I did, and I remained in that dress until the stylist told me her next appointment had arrived and it was time for me to go. This dress was the perfect opposite to what I had in mind and I loved it.

I didn't stop. I went to Bergdorf Goodman with my mom and sister to try on gowns I could never afford. I'm not sure I should recommend doing this. On the one hand, slipping into a $12,000 gown was so kind of amazing. On the other hand, what if I'd fallen in love with one of them? I knew that I wasn't wearing white, so I considered myself safe. For some women, trying on wedding gowns is a marvelously good time, so even if you know what you're wearing, don't skip this. Unless you hate it. Sam hates trying on clothes, hence why packages arrive at our door daily. Online shopping is her thing.

Anyway, back at Bergdorf's, some of the lace looked better on me than the Nicole Miller dresses, and one Vera Wang ball gown made five foot eleven me look like a toddler playing dress-up. That iconic Monique Lhuillier lace silhouette with the dramatic open back? I looked shapeless. Oh well.

After our appointment I dragged mom and sis down a few floors to the women's formal dress department. I grabbed a silk taffeta in emerald green, and though the cut wasn't quite what I was after, both my mom and sister could see the look on my face when I slipped into that dress. This was me. This color made me look and feel my best.

When I finally took my plans to my dressmaker, Kathryn Conover, I told her about this simple, perfect Nicole Miller gown. "But I want a deeper back," I explained, "And a green lace overlay." She was skeptical on this green lace. I explained that I wouldn't be wearing a veil and this lace, which I would remove post-ceremony, would give me that soft, feminine touch. Months passed and we made changes to the dress as Kathryn searched for green French lace—no easy feat. As the dress came together I periodically stopped by her showroom to wrap myself in silk-taffeta, swoon over lace, and ask her opinion on accessories. I loved every second of the experience of having a dress made just for me. I also learned that it's okay to know what you want and to stick to it. My wedding dress wasn't for everyone, but dammit, it was perfect for me.

Sam decided early on that she would probably wear Vera Wang. I didn't love the idea of her spending so much on a gown, but I wanted us both to feel our best on our wedding day. She wouldn't tell me the color of her dress or what it looked like, but I knew our dresses would be complementary. As someone who does not always love to wear dresses, she was drawn to the haphazard styles of Vera Wang gowns. She went to only two bridal appointments. Unlike me, she wanted to get this over with. It took her a few tries at Vera Wang and a sneaky aunt finding a dress in the back before she had the perfect gown.

The night before our wedding we wore white and asked guests to as well. I had a vision, of course, that took some time to pull together, but in the end I loved my look. I bought a low cut-off-white bodysuit with an open crisscross back and paired it with a long tulle skirt from Ann Taylor. I am still hoping that one of these days I'll have an event worthy of this skirt. The entire look cost about $350 and Sam says it's the most beautiful she's ever seen me. I do appreciate that, although the ensemble was inexpensive and I did my own hair and make-up, as opposed to our wedding day... Sam wanted a white jumpsuit, which, believe it or not, we could not find at the time. Finally, she came up with the next best thing. She paired a pair of white pants from Bloomingdale's with a white button down and a white Uniqlo blazer. My mom did her hair in a sock bun. She looked amazing.

That was only a few years ago, but today you need merely Google what you're looking for and it won't be long until you find it. What's even better? Those dresses we covet that are way out of our price range? You can have a custom version done for cheaper by a designer or fashion student. I took a friend dress shopping and her tiny frame and tanned, tattooed arms looked stunning in a silk slip dress that was wildly overpriced at over $7,000. "You can have that made for less than half," I told her. She did.

I remember when I was first engaged and friends would comment on the pale pink manicure I would need for my wedding day. I've never painted my nails light pink in my life and I certainly wasn't going to start now. Ya know what nail color makes me feel awesome? A really dark crimson, almost-raisin color. So that's the nail color I wore for my wedding. On your wedding day you don't want to look like someone else. A woman should feel like her best self on her wedding day. Whatever makes you feel beautiful is what you should wear, regardless of anyone's opinions or suggestions. I would have felt good in a white gown. I felt amazing in a green one. That worked for me and I don't regret it for a second. For some women, this means bare feet, for others, it means suspenders and cufflinks.

## EXPERT TIP:

*Kathryn Conover, Gown Designer*

### What's the biggest mistake you see brides making?

*I would not worry so much about the venue dictating the style. Obviously a gown that is long sleeved with a ball gown skirt for an outdoor July wedding could be problematic. But in general go with your heart in selecting a dress. And don't worry about pleasing everyone and worrying about what others think.*

*I would consult with one trusted advisor whose taste level you love, and then, of course, your wedding designer.*

### *Footwear, headwear, and other accessories*

Veils are beautiful. The veil-over-the-face trend may be no more, but a veil tucked into the back of your hair can look so glamorous. There are so many different kinds of veils, and chances are wherever you're dress shopping will have a nice stock of expensive veils. You'll be standing in front of the mirror eyeing yourself in this dress, telling your mom, sister, or best friend that you think you love this dress, and the stylist will walk up behind you and slide a comb into your hair, then spread the veil out across your back. She's hoping you'll cry. You might cry. Maybe you're that kind of bride. Fight this. Do not buy that veil! Hear me? That veil is too expensive. A veil, unlike a dress, does not require months of alterations. Choose a dress and then you have oodles of time to decide what to put on your head.

As I said, Sam wore her mother's headpiece from her 1981 wedding. She had it dyed to match her dress and it looked insanely beautiful on her. I didn't wear anything on my head or in my hair. Sometimes I think I should have but then I realize that my green dress with the lace overlay wasn't really in need of any accompaniment and besides, I'd spent a small fortune on hair color and extensions for my wedding and so I let them shine.

My sister-in-law wore something blue as a large blue flower in her hair. It looked amazing. My sister wore a brooch with a comb attached for her updo. My mom kept it and has gotten her money's worth, she wears it for pretty much every formal occasion. My friends have gone the route of traditional veils, some have gone veil-less, some have worn beaded hippie headbands around their foreheads. All have looked incredible, and so, so like themselves.

Footwear has been the same. Some brides go barefoot and sport toe rings. Some wear flats, some wear heels, and all should do what works for them. Try not to stress too much about finding the perfect pair of shoes. If your dress is long enough, chances are no one is going to see them. And if it's not, you can literally design your own shoes online, with a shoemaker, or take your time to find something pretty and comfortable. I wore a pair of sandals that I still wear. I'll be walking with a friend on a summer day and I'll look down and say, "These were my wedding shoes." And she'll laugh, because they don't look like wedding shoes, but they were perfect. And better yet, they were comfortable.

When it comes to your wedding look, my advice is to explore your options, then choose what feels right to you. And once you've decided, don't freak out. I haven't known a single bride who didn't face a panic. Sometimes it's months before the wedding, but months after she's chosen the dress. That image in her brain suddenly doesn't match up to the dress at her fitting. Sometimes there's something that needs to be fixed, or the second-guessing that comes with looking at other dresses and wondering, "Have I made a mistake?" You're not marrying the dress or the suit. Don't forget that. Trust yourself, and if that voice won't relent and you absolutely must change your mind, do not freak out, ask for help.

---

EXPERT TIP:

*Jill Hammelman, Hair Design*

**What's your number one budget insider-savings tip?**

*You can get fabulous hair bling on Etsy.*

- Wear a blue garter or blue underwear. If it works with your look, get a blue pedicure. (I had deep blue toenails. No one really saw my feet anyway and I thought it was fun and wedding-y.)
- Borrow jewelry. On our wedding day Sam wore a rose gold Cartier bracelet she'd gifted me on an anniversary. Borrowing from the other bride felt extra special. I wore a diamond ring that's a family heirloom and borrowed a bracelet from my sister.
- It's also fun to borrow hair accessories. One friend has had all the women in her family wear the same Swarovski hair clip.
- You shouldn't have trouble finding something new. Chances are your suit or dress is new, but if not, you can get new shoes, a pair of new earrings, or even a clip for your hair.
- If you're not wearing any family heirlooms and need something old, wear a pair of shoes you love or a piece of jewelry you've had forever.

*Other tips*

- Years ago I read on Martha Stewart that you should keep the excess fabric from bridesmaids dresses to wrap the bouquets. I took this one step further at my wedding and had Sam's bouquet wrapped in my fabric, and mine wrapped in hers. It added an extra layer to our first look, because once we had our bouquets the excitement really mounted.

- I had no intentions of changing my dress mid-wedding. I was in my dream dress and I was going to stay in my dream-dress until the sun came up. If you're looking to switch up your look from ceremony to reception, add or subtract something. I wore a lace overlay that I removed during the reception, and I added a funky Swarovski necklace. Some brides take their hair down for the party, and others lose the blazer and show off their custom suspenders.

- Break in your shoes! I had a terrible time finding shoes and finally settled on a simple pair of sandals. No one really saw them and I got to be comfortable. Sam, on the other hand, was in a stunning pair of sky-high Diane Von Furstenberg wedges. She had to practice walking in them. For weeks leading up to the wedding you might want to slip into your shoes for an hour each evening as you watch TV or do dishes. Your feet will thank you later.

- Get your undergarments in order. I was anti-Spanx for my wedding. I wanted to be able to wear regular undies and the bra that was built into my dress. If you're not certain what kind of bra you'll need with your dress, bring one to your last fitting. You do not want to be worrying about this on your wedding day.

- If you're doing hair and makeup then pack something comfortable. Maybe you have a bejeweled *Bride* tank, or maybe you're just going to wear sweats, but whatever it is don't wear a top that will mess up your look when you remove it.

- Think about temperature. If your dress is strapless and the forecast says it's going to be below forty with a wind chill, find a pretty wrap or coat to keep you warm during walks to and from photos. I love photos from winter weddings of brides in matching plaid wool wraps, or huddled under a chunky knit blanket. Sometimes keeping warm creates amazing photo ops.

- Additionally, if it's going to rain—but trust me, it won't—it's best to be prepared. Get a giant umbrella that reads "Mrs. & Mrs." when you open it, or get matching white rainboots for your walk to the venue. Nobody wants rain on her wedding day, but you can get some great photos out of uncooperative weather.

EXPERT TIP:

Daniel Friedman, Bindle and Keep Bespoke Suitmaker

**What's the first thing you ask new clients?**

*Before jumping into a discussion about fabric and color, we take the time to explore our clients' general relationship with clothing and their bodies. It's there where we gain the strongest sense of the type of suit and cut we should aim for. It's not uncommon for me to spend thirty minutes just discussing bust and hips, or more specifically, whether we should highlight or detract from what are often deeply emotionally sensitive areas of the body.*

*On your wedding day you want to look and feel like the best version of you*

# What to Pack

NOT GETTING READY AT home? Here's a packing guide with some obvious and not-so-obvious reminders.

### Clothing

- Your rehearsal outfit—clothing, shoes, accessories.
- Your wedding gown, suit, jumpsuit, skirt— whatever you're wearing on your wedding day. Make sure it's all in order. (If it needs to be steamed on-site you might have to pack a travel steamer.)
- Accessories—jewelry, veil or headpiece, scarf or coat, garter, and your handbag or clutch.
- Undergarments—wearing Spanx or something lacy beneath your gown? Don't forget it.
- Wedding night lingerie—I have a feeling I skipped this and saved it for the mini moon, but if you have something sexy to slip into post-nuptials, don't forget to pack it.
- Bathing suit, if applicable.
- Umbrella—it's better to be safe than sorry.
- Extra underwear. Because this is always a great suggestion.
- Lounge clothes. Even if you don't think you'll have any downtime, you will never regret bringing something comfy.

- Work-out clothes and sneakers. If you're up for it some exercise will help you feel your best.
- After-party attire. If there's any chance you'll want to change into something more comfortable, pack it.
- Morning-after outfit.
- Layers. Weather can be unpredictable.

### Toiletries

- Band-aids, cotton balls, Q-tips, and tampons.
- Prescription meds, vitamins, sleeping pills, allergy meds, antacids, and headache medicine.
- If you're wearing nail polish bring your color and a top coat in case you get nicked.
- Razor and shaving cream.
- Sunscreen.
- Your makeup. Just because you have a professional doesn't mean you won't have a few touch-up ideas of your own.
- Safety pins and bobby pins, if applicable, just in case.
- Breath mints and mouthwash.
- Floss (nobody wants to be the bride with food stuck in her teeth.)
- A gigantic water bottle, because back-up hydration never hurts.
- Lotions and potions—don't forget your shampoo and conditioner, body wash, lotion, baby powder, face wash, and moisturizer.
- Deodorant.
- Toothbrush and toothpaste.

- Hair dryer and styling tools. If you're doing your own hair and don't trust the hotel or room you're staying in, be safe and pack your own dryer.
- Perfume or cologne. My wife's favorite thing about me is my smell. I can honestly say I would have ruined our wedding day if I'd forgotten it.
- Lipstick—bring your favorite lip color in case you don't like what your makeup artist has.
- Wipes or a Tide stick.
- Straws. If you're drinking during makeup application you'll be glad you brought these.

**Other**
- Sunglasses. And regular glasses if you wear them. Or contacts.
- Phone charger.
- Your vows.
- Card and/or gift for your bride.
- Wedding bands.
- Gifts for bridal parties and cash tips for vendors.
- Display photos and any décor you're transporting yourselves.

If you're heading up to your wedding venue a few days earlier leave some house keys with someone you trust. This way if you've forgotten anything they can stop by and get it for you.

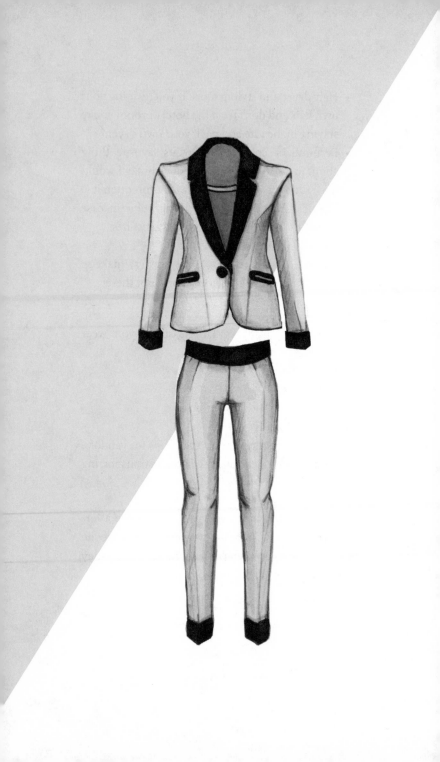

# Make An Entrance

**W**EDDINGS COME WITH A variety of traditions and etiquette. There are many performances, whether it's being given away by a father, or the receiving line in the back of the chapel. The newlywed entrance is another tradition that you can choose to enhance, ignore, or make all your own.

I've been in weddings where we are each paired up with a groomsman and individually announced. Some brides will ask you to perform in this moment. What does that mean? Oh, I bet you know. You've probably done it. They may want you and your groomsman to do a little dance. Maybe he'll twirl you. Maybe you'll go old school and raise the roof. Maybe you'll borrow my signature move and link arms while awkwardly waving your bouquet in the air. I get it. The entrance gets everyone pumped. The party is starting. Everyone's cheering. The newlyweds are almost here!!!

Maybe it's all the years working at a country club, but I cringe at hearing a DJ with a Long Island accent introduce people he's never met. I'm not sure why but I just assume all male DJ's have a Long Island accent. For one friend's wedding she had a large bridal party and we all simply stormed in together. The band was playing and everyone was cheering and we came in as one big group. No pressure, just excitement. I loved it. Some brides want to show off their wedding parties. Understandable, these men and women are our ride or dies, right? Chelsea and Cobina had all-female bridal parties. They invited the ladies to choose their own entrances. The brides describe their choices: "Two did a 'Tebow,' which is holding the back of their head and chugging a beer, two did squats (a hockey workout), two took selfies, two did a chest bump, two danced, two piggy-backed and then our maids-of-honor shotgunned."

Sam and I wandered into our reception along with our guests. We didn't want any big pronouncements. We'd already been declared wife and wife at the end of our ceremony, and we'd been hanging out with our guests at cocktail hour. Introductions were simply not necessary. I didn't care if that was traditional or abnormal or whatever. Do what feels right for you. Have fun with your entrance and make it as wild or discreet as you and your bride want.

# Seating Assignments

I T's TRUE. THIS IS one of those mundane tasks that only the most OCD brides actually enjoy. The dreaded table assignments.

Sam and I waited as long as absolutely possible to create our seating charts. We had a good idea of how this would go, because some of the seating arrangements are pretty obvious. Certain sides of the family go together as do particular groups of friends. The trouble comes when you have to split tables up. When you have to combine different groups of friends to complete tables. When you have a friend from grad school who knows almost no one at your wedding. When you have the couple for whom you used to nanny who don't know anyone, either. These are where things get tricky. Sure, you can put all the single people at one table. They might hate you for it. You can also try to get creative and split up all of your friends and mix and match everyone because you think it would be so nice if loved ones could branch out. Guess what? Nobody wants to branch out at your wedding. They want to hit the open bar, eat some food at a table with their own friends, and get super sweaty on the dance floor.

And then there are the weddings that lend themselves to open seating. If the entire event is one big cocktail party, or there's a buffet but everyone will be mingling, then you might skip the task of assigning seats altogether. But if you want tables reserved for parents or your wedding party, you may have to assign them yourselves.

There is also you and your bride to consider. If you want a sweetheart table then there's your solution. It's a safe bet that none of your guests will help themselves to the intimate table for two. Many couples end up at a sweetheart table simply to make the seating assignments easier. Other couples like having their own private perch from which to enjoy the festivities.

Sam and I did not want a sweetheart table at our wedding. We wanted to be right there in the middle of the excitement with our loved ones. We had a vision of one long, head table, with square tables surrounding. We didn't have bridal parties and our head table needed to be large. Our parents would be at separate tables with their friends. This left us wondering how to do the seating at our own table. Before we did too much over-thinking we reminded ourselves that this was not such a big deal. In the end we chose our siblings, some cousins, and a few of our closest friends who were featured in the ceremony or had traveled far distances to be with us.

We knew we would have to split up particular groups of friends. One group was just a couple people too big to share one table, so I had to move a few over. Again, when I started to stress about this I tried to remember what goes on at a wedding.

You sit in your seat for probably the first twenty to thirty minutes. You pick at a salad, you watch the brides dance, maybe they dance with their dads, too. Then a few speeches, and maybe dinner is served right away. For most of the time at your table you're *supposed* to be paying attention, so what does it matter who you're with? Once the dance floor is open then seating charts are abandoned and all bets are off. If your seating chart is making you crazy then just try to remember that this is not the end of the world. If a guest is really that angry you separated her from her college roommate then let her know it's best to suffer in silence.

If you have grandparents, handicapped guests, or anyone who might need special attention, it's best to consider them when creating your seating chart. Maybe Grandpa shouldn't be directly next to the band. Maybe Great Aunt Betsy should be close to a bathroom. If there's going to be a buffet try to ensure that the older crowd can access the food first. They generally think they deserve it and, really, they do.

Some guests might move their seats before they've even entered the ballroom. Don't let this bother you, either. Sure, it's rude. We're all adults and we can handle a seating assignment for an hour. But some people will do it anyway. So what? Go on with your good time.

One of the tables at our wedding got completely messed up. I still don't know how it happened, but strangers were combined and one table was missing most of its occupants. Sure, we felt bad about it. Was I going to let it ruin my night? Absolutely not.

---

**EXPERT TIP:**

*Breck Hofstedder, Sesame Letterpress*

### What's the first thing you ask new clients?

*We start by asking our clients to tell us about their wedding in general. It's helpful for us to be able to picture the event through their eyes and listen to the details they are excited about. The invitations offer guests the first glimpse of the celebration to come so it is important that the suite conveys this. While wedding invitations are formal in nature, most of our clients are not formal people. We like the invitations to be able to represent both the couple and the event so the more we know about the couple and what details of the wedding excite them, the more opportunities we have to personalize the invitation suite.*

# How do You Make a Great Speech at a Lesbian Wedding?

WHO SHOULD SPEAK AT your wedding? That really depends on what you and your bride want your wedding to be. Do you want to dance all night? Then you might not want ten people grabbing the microphone. Do you want to sit and eat dinner and listen to stories? Then maybe you do want to pass that mic around. If you have a best man, best woman, maid of honor, or whatever you choose to call them, it is customary that they make a speech. You can also ask parents or grandparents, or anyone else you'd like to hear from.

At my own wedding I wanted to celebrate. Sam and I chose to hear from both of our fathers as well as her brother and my sister. We got some great speeches and then we got on with the dancing. Decide how much time you're willing to spend on speeches during your reception, and keep in mind that each speaker can take about five to ten minutes.

If they don't know what to say, tell them this:

I'll start by sharing my Dad's advice for giving a speech: brevity.

This is great advice, as I've both given and witnessed many wedding speeches, and no one but the speaker really appreciates a speech that rambles on.

Two other things I've learned through experience: **write it down**. Trying to go off the cuff usually results in a repetitive speech that is longer than planned. I am a terrible public speaker. About 80 percent of my body turns bright red and I forget to breathe. I look and sound like I am having some sort of breakdown. So I always write it down. Even if I've tried to memorize what I'm saying, that little piece of paper can ground me, and yes, I even put little checks where I need to stop and breathe.

Finally, **don't use too many inside jokes or personal stories**. You risk alienating the audience. Certainly use some, and remember that you're speaking to a couple, not an individual, and there is likely a room full of guests politely listening. If your best friend asks you to speak at her wedding it's not a chance for you to tell all of your wildest college stories. Tell one that reveals something about her or about your friendship, then be sure your speech evolves to include her new spouse.

### Same-sex wedding speech advice

When planning my own wedding, I was hyper-aware that guests were talking about the "lesbian wedding," and I focused on making it less *lesbian* and more *wedding*. I was so focused, in fact, that I almost forgot that this was a same-sex wedding, and that we were incredibly fortunate to have such support from our loved ones. Finally, in my sister Katy's maid of honor speech, she reminded all of us what we were celebrating. In this way I think her speech was perfect.

Katy didn't just give an incredible MoH speech, which was poignant and funny and candid, but she also took the opportunity to acknowledge what we were all here to celebrate. This was a same-sex wedding and here we were, in a candlelit barn filled with our nearest and dearest. There were many different kinds of people in that room, from my eighty-eight-year-old conservative grandfather (who always ended every phone call with "love you both") to Sam's Jewish aunts, our colleagues, childhood friends and glam gay best friends, and many of our college sorority sisters. Every single one of them was there with love and support for us. We never once, over the course of planning this wedding, had to worry that someone might disapprove, or that a family member wouldn't show up. Everything about planning this wedding felt normal. It felt right to plan a wedding so that I could marry the person I love, and it felt right to include all of these beautiful people, and this was worth acknowledging. My sister ended her speech with these lines:

*This is a real life modern family. The rest of the world is very slowly learning what we here have already known for years, that love is love. A family can be comprised of so many parts but in the end it's love and friendship that holds it all together. Laura and Sam, congratulations, I wish you all the happiness in the world and love you both dearly.*

She had to pause for a moment when she said "love is love," as the entire wedding had erupted in big, boisterous applause. It was worth saying, and worth noticing, that in this room we didn't see ourselves as different. We saw ourselves as family.

If you want to say a few words at your own wedding you can also keep it short. There's no reason to name names unless you're thanking your in-laws for hosting the rehearsal dinner or your parents for throwing the wedding, otherwise you can thank your guests for being a part of your special day and take this opportunity to let them know that their support means the world to you and your bride.

# Wedding Song

I AM JUST GOING to get this out of the way. I have serious opinions about wedding songs. Time and time again I hear couples using the same songs that were hits at the time of their wedding planning and I always cringe just a little. I get it, maybe a cheesy or wildly overplayed song has accidentally yet profoundly come to represent something between the two of you, and like it or not you know this is YOUR song, as much as it's the song of about half a million other couples this year. This is okay. And I apologize for any obvious snark, but if you can help it, dig a little deeper.

Some couples have it easy. Julie and Laura met at the jukebox of a dive bar, when Julie reached over Laura to play Miley Cyrus's "See You Again." The rest, they say, was history, and of course, this was their wedding song. Jenna and Betsy can't remember when "Kiss the Girl" from *The Little Mermaid* became *their* song, but it stuck.

Some lesbian couples don't have a first dance (I didn't) and so we're left wondering:

### What song is the wedding song?

I'm not positive that my wife and I agree on our wedding song. I think it's our processional, but we did have a private, romantic, post-ceremony dance that she planned secretly, so maybe she would say that the one we danced to is our song. There's also the first song that we ever agreed we both liked—we had very different tastes in music when we met—and not only did we name one of our dogs after that band, Ludo, but we had our sister-in-law read some of the lyrics during our ceremony. There's also the song we fell in love with many months after our wedding and used in our wedding video. So what's our wedding song? I believe they all are.

- Processional: "Heavenly Day"—Patty Griffin
- Recessional: "I Kissed a Girl" (Acoustic)—Katy Perry
- Private mountaintop dance: "Crazy Love"—Van Morrison
- Wedding video: "Bonfire Heart"—James Blunt

When I was younger my dad played me Patty Griffin and I fell in love with her music. I've seen her perform live and I generally think that every song she's ever written is brilliant. Once Sam and I had booked our venue and chosen our ceremony spot, each time I listened to "Heavenly Day" I pictured walking down the aisle toward Sam. I'd played it for her before, but this time I said, "Listen. I think it's perfect." She agreed.

Katy Perry's "I Kissed a Girl," on the other hand, was a popular pop song, a silly anthem about bicurious youth, and Sam and I agreed that it was the perfect nod to our sorority past. We also agreed that this was the perfect way to end the ceremony. The slowed down acoustic version fit in with the mood of the day, while the song signaled *it's party time!*

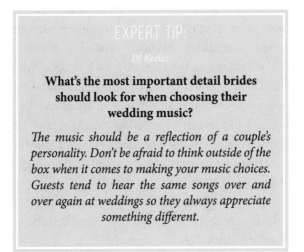

EXPERT TIP:

*DJ Keelez*

**What's the most important detail brides should look for when choosing their wedding music?**

*The music should be a reflection of a couple's personality. Don't be afraid to think outside of the box when it comes to making your music choices. Guests tend to hear the same songs over and over again at weddings so they always appreciate something different.*

*So here's the next question—do you have a first dance?*

I've seen someone laugh at a photo of two women in wedding gowns dancing together. I know it can appear a little awkward, but for some couples the first dance is the most romantic part of their wedding, and we know better than to plan two-bride weddings worried about what people think looks weird or funny or awkward. As I said, Sam and I had a private post-ceremony dance on a mountaintop. It was a romantic surprise she had planned because we were not having a first dance. There were a few reasons for this. First, we are just not that kind of couple. Vows and kissing in front of our loved ones was a big beautiful deal, but we weren't going to slow dance, too. I also tend to get antsy at weddings and spend most of the first dance, father/daughter mother/son dances standing around at the bar. We were dancing the Hora and both dancing with our fathers, plus they were both speaking and we had maid of honor and best man speeches. That seemed like plenty of wedding tradition and we wanted the rest of the reception to be about having fun, listening to great music, eating great food and drinking cocktails.

Okay, so if you don't have an obvious song—or at least not one that feels appropriate for a wedding—then how do you choose a song?

### You listen to music!

- Do you have a favorite band that you've both seen live more times than you can count? Do they have a song that might work with your wedding?
- Is there a song you listened to constantly when you first met? If it's too upbeat, would an acoustic version be perfect for your recessional?
- Were you both born the same year? Any hit love songs from then?

- Do you want a tongue-in-cheek first dance? Maybe the Indigo Girls, Melissa Etheridge, or a little Tegan & Sara work for you.
- Do you know a popular love song that's been covered by a band you love? Or maybe there's an acoustic version that's more sentimental?

The best bet is to call your DJ or get in touch with your band. Find out what they recommend. They eat, sleep, and breathe music. If you're looking for a soulful power ballad, they'll point you in the right direction. If you want to unearth a romantic song by The Zombies, they'll help you do it. It's totally okay to ask for help and listen to different kind of music to see what fits you as a couple, and what works with the vibe of your wedding.

# Booze Rules

I HAD BEEN GIVEN stern warning by no fewer than five people not to drink too much at my wedding. An out and proud party girl, I can go from zero to wild in no time at all, and worried loved ones didn't want me to look back at my wedding photos and see nothing but drunk face. I heard their concerns, and I reminded them that I was no fool. "If I'm old enough to get married, I'm old enough to handle myself like an adult." Guess what? I was perfectly behaved. Well, I mean, I didn't get out of control, and by the time I really let loose the after-party was in full swing and everyone was under a variety of influence so I fit right in.

How did I do it, you ask? Easy. I love to have a drink in my hand. I knew that once the party started it would be tough for me to abstain, so I had the bartenders keep a bottle of Aperol on hand. I drank Aperol and soda for the first few hours. It was yummy, super low in alcohol, and quite a lovely color.

So here's the deal. No one bothered talking to Sam about these things. She rarely drinks enough to get tipsy, let alone drunk, but for me, there were plans in place. I sipped my Aperol and soda for most of the evening and I always had water at hand. I also ate food. Crazy right? Along with passed desserts like miniature milk and cookies, tiny cups of coffee with donuts and mashed ginger ice cream, we had passed shots. Sam loves tequila and I—with no shame at all—love whipped cream–flavored vodka. We had trays of both circulating the room. I look back at the photos now and see Sam throwing back tequila with many, many of our wedding guests.

I wasn't sure how much Sam was drinking, but I assumed she was staying in control. After we cut our cake together and posed for a few photos I made my way back to the dance floor and we lost each other. We'd dance around for a bit, find each other, smooch, then disappear into the crowd. Suddenly it was the end of the wedding. Our wedding planner was signaling me that it was time for our sparkler exit so we could move everyone to the after-party location. I looked for Sam and spotted her across the room at a table with her aunt. I approached. "It's not good," Sam's aunt repeated as she spooned cake into Sam's mouth. I looked hard at my wife's face and noticed her huge eyes had no focus at all. I'd never seen her this drunk. "Hey, Babe." I touched her back shoulder. "We need to do the sparkler exit." It took a few more minutes of pleading until finally I grabbed her and told her to hold onto me and just keep her mouth shut.

Some people were already on their second sparklers by the time we were ready to walk out. We'd taken so long to exit. We walked, our arms around each other's backs, smiles on our faces, though her eyes were rolling in every direction.

Everyone cheered as I wondered just how my bride was going to make it to our after-party. The few pictures of the sparkler exit look great. In the images we are walking out of the barn and into a dark night, through showers of flame with our arms around each other. Really, I'm holding onto her for dear life because I am worried that Sam will fall or, worse, wander off. Ahh, newlyweds. In my vows I assured Sam, "Our union may not be perfect, but it will be raucous and unruly and perfectly us." This was already turning out to be true.

I've heard other stories like this one. One bride had to be put to bed by friends in the first hour of her wedding reception. She was inconsolable the following day. I knew I would never forgive myself if that happened to me, but I'm also not mad at my wife for getting the drunkest and craziest I've ever seen her. She had the time of her life. When I initially saw the level of Sam's inebriation I was sad because I thought she would miss the after-party we'd planned. We had been so excited for this part of the night. Somehow, and this is a mystery to me, she pulled it together. After a quick stop in our room to change her out of her dress, Sam was running around the after-party in girls-gone-wild zombie style. The party got totally out of hand, went all night long, and we wouldn't have had it any other way.

# The Grand Finale

**B**ACK IN THE DAY the newlyweds would disappear from their wedding reception, presumably consummating the marriage or heading off on their honeymoon. The bride would be in a smart, sensible jumpsuit or pencil skirt and the party, I imagine, would continue after their departure.

This is no longer the norm. Sure, it's still done. I've attended a wedding where the bride and groom waved goodbye and off they went. These days, however, more often than not, the newlyweds are the last to go. If it's not the latter, then they're leaving the venue with their bridal parties perhaps, or boarding buses to their after-party. One word of advice is to have a plan. Back in my country club days we were rolling tables within twenty minutes of the wedding ending. I always felt kinda bad if the bride was still hanging out, savoring the last few moments of her big day, but it was late, we were tired, and the party was over. The point is, don't be that bride hanging around after the magic has diffused.

*A grand exit works for two reasons:*
- It gets everyone out of the venue
- It creates photo opportunities

Sam and I went with sparklers. Why? We were in the middle of the woods. It was walk-face-first-into-a-tree dark out there and sparklers lit up our exit for, you guessed it, the photos. They also gave everyone a little pyro thrill, not to mention let them get their bearings with a few moments of light.

If you're not in the dark there's always confetti or bubbles. You can go old school and have your guests throw rice, or you can be creepy and have everyone release butterflies.

Hey, what about a second line? I've mentioned these a few times because I am obsessed with New Orleans and seriously, what's better than a brass band parade just for you? If your after-party or next stop is within walking distance then why not get there in style?

If you're less worried about the exit and more about ending the wedding then think about a great song to end the night with. Get everyone wild on the dance floor and go out with a bang. Maybe you and your fiancée already have a song you go wild for, or maybe your entire family is smitten with one awesomely bad pop song. There are great eighties power ballads, with which you can never go wrong. Years ago a group of girlfriends and I fell hard for Enrique Iglesias' "I Like It." Seriously, we scream "fiesta forever" like it's actually the last fiesta of our lives. As we all get plucked up and married off that song is a number one wedding request and the best way to get all of us in cahoots on the dance floor.

You can also opt for a slow dance. Maybe it's time for everyone to power down. Regardless, it never hurts to have a plan.

And here's one more tip: munchies. If the after-party is a trek away or you're not doing a formal party with food, then sending guests off with some grub is an awesome way to end the night. Alex and Tawnie had an In-N-Out truck outside of their Pacific Palisades wedding and it was a hit with locals and out-of-towners alike. Food trucks may be trendy but one thing that trumps trend is function: most guests will be ready for a bite to eat. Besides, your wedding diet is over, time to enjoy! You can also have guests take home sweets, like cookies packaged to go as a parting gift. Leave a cute note about how sweet love is and voila! Everyone's happy.

# After-Party

TODAY THE AFTER-PARTY IS as much a wedding staple as cocktail hour. It's all but expected, but luckily, it can be as low-key or extravagant as you newlyweds want.

I, for instance, was married in the middle of nowhere. There would be no hotel room cocktails or late-night jukebox dancing in a dive bar. For those guests who made it to midnight with their wits intact, the reward was an after-party with delicious food—think buffalo chicken sliders and grilled cheese—a great DJ, a bonfire for those who were ready to wind down, and a free-for-all of booze for guests to serve themselves. This meant my drunk friends made me some concoction in a plastic cup, which I poured out and replaced with an entire two-liter bottle of whipped cream vodka. I carried that bottle around my after-party, sipping and stopping to pour its contents down the throats of friends and family, including my best friend's parents and one of Sam's aunts. This is what separated our wedding from our after-party: The wedding retained some semblance of class. the after-party was a free-for-all, no-holds-barred blow-out. I stayed in my gown, by the way, because if you're going to get married in your dream dress, then you don't change out of it. You wear this thing one time. Make it count.

For my friend who got married in New Orleans we made a stop at her favorite dive bar—which made for great photos of the bride—then there was a laidback, change-out-of-your-dresses-and-suits party in the hotel courtyard. One room was used as the bar—rumor has it there was champagne and beer in their bathtub for days. Speakers were hooked up to an iPod, pizzas were ordered, and there was a party.

A friend in Tribeca made the drunken walk with guests over to an old haunt where we commandeered the jukebox and pool table, and a friend who got married on Fire Island simply extended the wedding so nobody had to leave. My brother's wedding ended with an impromptu gathering at the bride's mother's house. There are many possibilities to fit every style and budget.

Some brides want a black tie wedding but then, while they have their best friends surrounding them, want to get down and dirty in their favorite bar. Others invite their closest circle back to the honeymoon suite for late-night cocktails and snacks, and some just hit the hotel bar. Whatever you want to do, it's best to plan ahead of time. This doesn't meant spending money or making reservations, but if your plan is to hit the hotel bar, for instance, check ahead of time that they'll be open and able to accommodate your party size.

EXPERT TIP:

*Lisa Karvellas, Owner & Chef at Cedar Lakes Estate*

**What's your most frequent request?**

*People love drunk munchies at the after-party! I think it's because the wedding diet is finally over, so the bride wants to make sure there's a greasy cheeseburger and French fries waiting for her as soon as she exits the reception.*

### Some Dos and Don'ts

- If you're keeping it VIP, don't start chatting about the exclusive after-party during your wedding. Uninvited guests will inevitably find out and feel terrible.

- Similarly, don't invite a small group on a separate bus. If you're keeping it VIP then scoot the bridal party back into the limo and head out.

- If you want to party at another location but guests will need their own transportation, talk to a cab company ahead of time so everyone is guaranteed a safe ride.

- If you're having people back at your place get it set up beforehand. Keep it simple: leave booze and cups on the counter and easy-to-serve snacks like dips in the fridge. Better yet—order pizzas. Have a playlist ready to go on your iPod and you've got a party.

- Hosting the party wherever you're staying means no transportation for you when you've had enough, but it might also mean guests hanging around late-night when you've had enough. Maybe your maid of honor is open to hosting some friends back in her room and you can slip out when you're ready.
- If you have a large group and you're heading to a bar or restaurant it's best to call ahead so they're ready to accommodate you.
- Keep this in mind: if you don't want to see another bride (beside your own) on your wedding day, then avoid a public place. We've all arrived at a hotel bar only to find another woman in white exchanging judgey glances with our best friend. I was determined on my wedding day that my wife and I would be the only two brides on the planet. I don't always play well with others.
- Whatever you do, make sure there's food. Chances are you and your guests have been imbibing for hours, so whether it's light snacks or a catered meal, make sure there's something available.
- If there's money left in your budget for an after-party, consider asking your reception venue if they can host it. Perhaps they can move you to a smaller room for drinks and snacks, or maybe your DJ can stay an extra hour. Staying put ensures you don't lose the people you've hoping to spend more time with.

Two Advil before bed and see you in the morning!

# Consummating the Marriage

I'M ALWAYS A LITTLE shocked, and I almost always scoff when my friends tell me they are wholly committed to having sex on their wedding night. Let me just start by saying there was no sex on my wedding night—at least not between myself and my bride, I'm sure plenty of our guests were having drunken romps all over the venue grounds. Not only did we not have sex, we had no plans to have sex. This had been a real discussion, right up there with "should we do a sparkler exit?" (We did.)

Here's why: whether you're having a big blowout or an intimate gathering, if you're inviting guests then this is likely the only time in your lives that you will have this carefully selected group of people together to celebrate your marriage. That's it! Do you really want to waste any of this time together doing the thing that you've probably been doing together for years now and will certainly be doing for years to come? For Sam and I the answer was: hell no!

I was staying in that damn dress until the sun came up. I was going to rage with my loved ones until the last guest stumbled away to their cabin. I wasn't going to miss a minute of this. We'd sunk countless hours and insane amounts of money into our wedding celebration and I was going to enjoy every second of it. That's not to say I wasn't enamored with my bride, because I was thrilled that we officially belonged to each other forever, but with a honeymoon still to come, the wedding night was for celebrations with loved ones.

I mean, isn't this what honeymoons are all about? Spending time together, just the two of you, relaxing, making love, generally enjoying every ounce of each other? I'd guess that for most couples wedding night sex results in sloppy we-didn't-even-finish mediocrity.

Brides Roxanne and Jenny were so consumed with making sure their destination wedding went off without a hitch that they didn't dwell on the thought of having sex on their wedding night. Consummating the marriage is, after all, an antiquated tradition in which the virgin bride gives herself—entirely—to her husband…and we're not about that, are we?

The truth is that it's nobody's business. Do it or don't do it, but don't feel pressured from anyone outside of your new marriage. If anyone asks, tell them to bugger off, but I'm here to tell you that sex on your wedding night—no matter how you choose to do it—is not a required element of the wedding.

# The Morning After

THE SUNDAY BRUNCH AFTER my wedding was a sorry bunch of people sipping orange juice or coffee and nursing hangovers. But me, I'd been on my best behavior. I'd been the perfect bride—well, close enough—and I was ready to party. I wrangled my few friends who could keep down alcohol and decided we would finish off the wedding kegs. I got in the lake for some ziplining and blobbing, both of which I'd had the foresight not to do on my wedding day. While everyone else was getting organized and cleaning up, I was letting loose. It was so much fun. And I really don't feel that bad for not helping clean up.

Many of your guests will have early flights or long rides home. Not everyone will want to get together, but something as simple as bagels and juice is a nice way to say thank you and goodbye to your loved ones. If no one is jumping at the chance to host your post-wedding brunch, you can simply make plans with your friends who are not rushing off, or if yours is a destination wedding, choose a favorite restaurant or bar for one more drink. Roxanne and Jenny chose a cute little dive bar with great ocean views so everyone at their destination wedding could gather to reminisce about their time together and toast to safe travels. If all of your guests are staying at the same hotel or resort, have a brunch on location, or meet everyone at the pool for cocktails and recovery. It's great fun to recap the fun that's been had and share those final hugs and kisses before everyone takes off and you embark on a honeymoon or head home to married life.

# Gifts & Thank You Cards

I T'S PRETTY CRAZY AS adults to open this many gifts at once. It's also crazy to realize how many people love you, and in some cases, go over and above for you. Wedding gifts will make you feel kinda weird but immensely grateful at the same time.

### Here are some tips and reminders

#### Stay organized

- An Excel spreadsheet or lined notebook is your best friend here. Keep track of who got you what. It's always a nice touch to mention both how happy you were to have them in attendance and how psyched you are to cook steaks and use your new knife set.

#### Thank everyone

- Yes, it's tacky, but you might have wedding guests who inexplicably come empty handed. Okay, so not everyone got you a gift. That's not the end of the world, but it's hard to believe there are guests who would show up without a card, but there are. You still need to send a thank you card to every guest in attendance. They may not have any etiquette, but you do. Additionally, many guests will mail a card or gift later, so while I know there are brides who have their thank you notes written before the ink on their marriage license is dry, this is one instance when it pays to wait. If waiting isn't your thing, it's okay to thank everyone prematurely. So many guests at my wedding partied so hard they forgot to slip their cards into the rustic card crate provided. They mailed them to me the following week, which was fun all in itself. Some time later, as a bridesmaid in one of my best friend's weddings, I drank so much that I too opened my clutch the next day to find the card still in my possession. It happens to the best of us.

### No, you can't ask for the receipt

- Some guests will go rogue and send you stuff you didn't register for. Maybe these gifts will be an aesthetic very opposite of your taste. You can re-gift these items. You can donate them to Goodwill. You can even attempt to return for store credit. You cannot, under any circumstances, ask for a receipt. That's right, you'll send an enthusiastic thank you card and move on.

### Don't lose the checks

- Just as you can't ask for a receipt, I'm a pretty firm believer that you can't go asking your cousin Janet to write you a new check because you've misplaced hers in the throes of wedding packing. If you're going to open all of your cards while you're still at your wedding venue, hotel, or destination, then be sure to keep all checks and gift cards in an envelope in a secure place. Better yet, collect all gifts and cards and pack them right away.

### Don't stress if you can't get your thank you cards out right away

- You don't need to have cards in the mail the week after your wedding. But if six months have passed then it's time to pick a Saturday night, stay in, and write those cards. You don't have to write a novel. You do have to say thanks

### Order cards with a printed message

- Of course I wanted to use one of our breathtaking wedding photos for our thank you cards. I had the date printed inside as well, but sometimes I think we should have printed a thank you message in there as well. Of course you still have to address and sign them, but if some of your guests were parents' friends, for instance, you don't need to get too personal

### Cards should be mailed

- Even if your wedding invitation was a Paperless Post your thank you cards should be actual cards that are signed, stamped, and mailed to their recipients

# POST-WEDDING CHECKLIST:

☐ If you haven't completed your name-change documents yet, make an appointment at the DMV and get this done so it's not nagging at you.

☐ Open your gifts and keep everything organized. The sooner you take care of your thank-yous the better you'll feel. But don't stress too much, it's not abnormal to take a couple of months.

☐ Check in with your venue and make sure you haven't left anything behind and that you don't have any outstanding invoices.

☐ Make arrangements to clean and/or preserve your wedding gown. If you're planning to wear everything again, have it dry cleaned ASAP. Fabric tends to get absolutely destroyed at weddings.

☐ Update your social media so everyone knows you just had the best wedding ever and you're taken.

☐ Plan a honeymoon if you're not already on it.

☐ Live happily every after.

# Honeymoon

IN A 2015 PIECE for *Cosmopolitan* magazine I told the story of my honeymoon, how we traveled to Southeast Asia for nearly three magical weeks. Before we left my wife studied up. "No kissing," she warned me, "but we can hold hands. They'll think we're just friends." I didn't stop to think how ridiculous it was to go on a honeymoon and pretend it was something else. I didn't think about how we would be cheating ourselves by behaving as something that we weren't. We're not a couple who do too much canoodling in public, so offensive behavior was never on the table. I thought that by day we would be tourists and safely behind closed doors in our hotel suites we'd be newlyweds.

The first leg of our trip was great. We stayed in plush, king-size beds. We took bubble baths and sipped local beer at dinner, and when our tour guide in Siem Reap, Cambodia, asked too many questions, we played coy, never quite admitting the nature of our relationship. Then we flew to Bangkok, and a plump lady in pigtails greeted us in a screeching lisp, her Hello Kitty manicure catching my eye as she clapped her hands in delight. "Happy Honeymoon," she repeated before turning to my wife, "And your birthday is coming!" I whispered to Sam in the back of our town car, "How does she know all this?"

We were using two different travel companies for the trip, and for the second half of our travels we'd been outed.

I am so very grateful that we were. We all plan to have only one honeymoon, right? So make it count. Enjoy the honeymoon perks—the rose petals in the bath, chocolates on the bed, and bubbly on ice. You deserve it and and I can tell you from experience, you'll feel so very special.

### My Honeymoon Advice

If you're taking a long, adventurous honeymoon, I absolutely recommend waiting a few months between your wedding and honeymoon. My wife and I were exhausted in the days following our wedding. I'm pretty sure a flight across the world would have killed us. Instead we got to focus on the wedding as one wonderful event, then turn our full attention to our honeymoon months later. Now, if you're hopping a plane to Mexico for a week of sun, sand, and relaxation, than going directly after your wedding may be the perfect plan. Go somewhere that feels special to both of you, whatever your budget, and let them pamper you. I nearly learned the hard way that champagne on ice and rose petals on your bed are one cliché you don't wanna miss.

Don't overplan. Even if your destination involves a lot of tourist attractions, make time for some newlywed time. Get a couples' massage, enjoy the Jacuzzi tub in your room, or lounge around in bath robes on your terrace. These are moments just for you, for romance and relaxation.

### Honeymoon Advice From a Pro

I spoke to John Tanzanella, President/CEO of the International Gay & Lesbian Travel Association

*What is the first piece of advice you give same-sex couples looking to plan a honeymoon?*

To do their homework on destinations. Check our website (www.IGLTA.org) to see if they are engaging in LGBT tourism. Look into the laws and cultures of the destination.

*Are there any destinations you advise couples to avoid?*

We never tell anyone to "not" go anywhere, as LGBT travelers want to see the world just like anyone. We must, however, be mindful of laws and cultural conditions.

*Do you suggest any dos and don'ts once couples have chosen a honeymoon destination? Can you give any examples?*

It can be helpful to find an LGBT travel agency, meeting planner to assist with details that they may not be aware of, particularly when it comes to destinations that may not be as welcoming as others. IGLTA offers travel agents specialized in LGBT tourism for their assistance.

*What is the benefit of using a travel agency that specializes in same-sex travel?*

They are more familiar with destinations, hotels, and vendors to help make the special event a success. Our travel agent members are the most versed on successful LGBT tourism and understanding the intricacies in this segment.

*Are destination choices different between gay men and women?*

There is overlap within both segments as they aren't so distinctive between where each group likes to travel. We have to delve more into each gender to see if they prefer adventure, city, relaxation, etc. That said, some destinations such as Provincetown, MA, have specific weeks of tourism targeting groups such as LGBT Family Week, Womens Week, Bear Week, etc.

*What are the top destination trends for lesbian couples?*

Lesbian couples are very cognizant of destinations and businesses that are marketing specifically to lesbians.

*Any budget-saving tips?*

Shop around and use IGLTA members. We have a range of businesses from budget to luxury. www.iglta.org

*Many same-sex couples have the story of being given separate beds in hotel rooms—any tips on how to avoid these awkward travel moments?*

Using an IGLTA travel agent or tour operator can help ensure you receive the appropriate room situation. They are knowledgeable on handling same-sex couples.

*Should couples feel comfortable traveling anywhere in the USA?*

They should but there are different feelings around the country that same-sex couples should be mindful of and ensure they don't put themselves into a position of discrimination or worse.

*Do you see many same-sex couples planning destination weddings?*

Yes, this is a growing area of same-sex weddings, particularly with newer couples as they want to experience the same life event their heterosexual friends have done. With same-sex couples that have been together for years, or even decades, its probably less important to have a destination wedding as it is to sign the legality of papers.

*What are the top honeymoon locations chosen by same-sex couples?*

It's a wide range of types of destinations just like in the straight community. Florida, Hawaii, NYC, Vegas, and New England are all in the top areas but the list is quite extensive depending on what the couple is looking for in their honeymoon experience. Many of the same-sex weddings so far have been among couples that have actually been together for many years, so the honeymoon isn't as significant as it would be with newly engaged couples.

*What's your stance on exclusively gay-friendly resorts?*

We love promoting these IGLTA member properties as there is no guess work for same-sex couples in their bed situations. There are some destinations with high concentrations of exclusively gay resorts such as Provincetown, Fort Lauderdale, and Palm Springs.

*When my wife and I took our honeymoon to Southeast Asia she told me, "No kissing or being affectionate in public!" But when we arrived at each destination not only did our tour guides and resort staff know we were on our honeymoon, they were all so gracious and kind. Do you find many couples are surprised at how well they're treated?*

Yes, we hear this often, particularly with consumers using an IGLTA member abroad. As IGLTA members they expect our travelers coming to them to be same-sex couples or LGBT individuals.

**It's worth noting** that I did not use a travel agency that specializes in LGBT travel, but we did share the nature of our trip with our travel professionals. If your chosen agency doesn't specialize in LGBT travel, they may still have great contacts to make your trip a success. Don't be afraid to ask questions and seek their recommendations and advice. And if you're not using a travel agent at all, bring any concerns to your resort concierge.

# What Would You Change?

**E**VERY SINGLE WEDDING THAT I publish on my website includes this question. I genuinely want to know if there's anything a couple would change about their wedding. Would they have splurged on that band they really wanted? Would they have nixed some of the endless desserts? Maybe they would have bagged the whole idea and eloped. I ask because I believe this question will help other brides.

Almost every single couple provides the same answer: "We wouldn't change a thing."

I call bullshit.

Okay, okay. I don't really, because it's true. Looking back on my wedding overall, there's nothing I would change. It was as close to perfect as possible, better than I ever imagined, and it was all around the greatest weekend of my life. I have, however, learned a few things. That's the beauty of hindsight. So as much as I appreciate when couples swear their wedding was perfect, I believe we each have a detail or two we would have done differently.

Here's mine: I'm impatient when it comes to anything I don't want to do. Take pictures for instance. In regular life I obsess over taking iPhone photos everywhere Sam and I go, and I post our pics on social media. But when it came to our wedding day I did not want to waste time on photos. I wanted to play and enjoy myself. I agreed to about an hour of pre-wedding photos and a very few post-ceremony. That was it. Let me be clear, the photos we have are incredible. Our photographer Heather Waraksa captured the spirit of our weekend entirely, but I probably should have given her more time. As it was we did not take full advantage of the venue and I wish I had more photos with some family and close friends in a few different locations. The good news is that we splurged on having her present Friday night as well, so that we have some stunning images from the night before our wedding, as well as the pre-ceremony festivities on our wedding day.

One couple shared with me that while their wedding was beautiful, their ceremony was a little disorganized. They say they should have insisted that their officiant help them re-draft the ceremony, rather than stick with what they had. They admit that because they ignored their instincts the ceremony was not as streamlined as they would have liked.

Another couple says they kept their wedding small and intimate, but in hindsight they feel that some very special people were missing from their big day. They admit they should have figured out a way to include everyone they loved.

More than one couple has admitted that they should have asked for help. I know I didn't ask for enough of it. There's the help of family and friends, and then there's help you pay for. With loved ones, so long as you're not being a bridezilla and you're openly grateful to them, they're usually willing to help. I've had many couples tell me that they should have hired a day-of coordinator. Planning can be fun until your wedding day, when you'd rather be enjoying the moment than worrying about whether the programs made it to the ceremony spot, or someone remembered to bring a cushion for Grandpa's chair. A day-of coordinator will handle all these little details without you having to worry. The best coordinators will even deal with any hang-ups or issues without you or your bride ever knowing about them.

The beauty of working with professional vendors is that they're experts. It's also your wedding, your money, your decision. Let your vendors and loved ones offer suggestions and guidance, but always follow your instincts. And ask for help.

One more piece of advice, if you haven't already gleaned this from previous pages: don't drink too much.

In the end we cannot dwell on the hiccups. The goal is to embark on a beautiful marriage and look back on your wedding as a spectacular kick-off. So many people and such various experiences and circumstances shaped my relationship with Sam. We've lived through heartache that we've caused for each other, and heartache caused by life and its circumstances. I often dispense unsolicited relationship advice, but what do I know for sure is that I married the only person I've ever loved. That's something I would never change.

# Author's Note

CONGRATULATIONS! YOU DID IT. You're married. This is what you've been waiting for. This is what all that planning and spending was about and I hope you took some advice but also trusted yourselves and threw a wedding that both you and your guests will remember for years to come.

Weddings are an industry, and it's easy to get caught up in the drama of the thing, but we out there who execute a two-bride wedding know that the commitment we're making is something extra special. Who we are is not a choice, and who we love is not always a choice either, but respecting the sanctity of our vows, and surrounding our marriage with the people who love and support us, that is a choice. It's a choice worth making. There are too many same-sex couples in this country and across the world who are persecuted and demonized. As we add our voices to the cries for equality, it is also worth noting our own good fortune.

Celebrating our marriages and being visible is an act in itself. So celebrate your relationship, your wedding, your marriage. Don't let anyone define these things for you. Find your other half and love her privately, publicly, and entirely.

### Resources

The following is a list of websites, companies, and publications that I have found helpful in the wedding planning process. Inclusion in this list does not imply endorsements or recommendations. These websites may change over time, and it's possible they are different from the time of this guide's printing. Visit 2brides2be.com for our complete list of preferred vendors.

#### Wedding planning and inspiration

- 2brides2be.com
- greenweddingshoes.com
- marthastewartweddings.com
- nymag.com/weddings
- offbeatbride.com
- rkbridal.com
- stylemepretty.com
- theknot.com/gay-lesbian-weddings
- *The Offbeat Bride* by Ariel Meadow Stallings
- *Your Wedding Your Way* by Sharon Naylor

#### Accessories and footwear

- bhldn.com
- davidsbridal.com
- dvf.com
- etsy.com
- katespade.com
- mariaelenaheadpieces.com
- nicolasacicero.com
- ninashoes.com
- nordstrom.com/c/wedding-accessories
- renttherunway.com

- shoesofprey.com
- toms.com
- zappos.com

## Beauty

- blissworld.com
- bumbleandbumble.com
- elizabetharden.com
- esteelauder.com
- jeffreysteinsalons.com
- jillhammelmanhairdesign.com
- lipsandlocks.com
- maccosmetics.com
- makeupfirst.com
- onceuponabride.net
- sb-beauty.net/photos/bridal
- sephora.com
- thedrybar.com

## Bridalwear

- anntaylor.com
- bhldn.com
- bindleandkeep.com
- blushbridalsarasota.com
- davidsbridal.com
- jandhp.com
- jcrew.com/wedding
- kathrynconover.com
- kleinfeldbridal.com
- knotstandard.com
- lovelybride.com
- macys.com
- renttherunway.com

- stevenbirnbaumbridal.com
- synderela.com
- verawang.com

## Design and Planning

- firefly-events.com
- ilanaashleyevents.com
- oshiflowers.com
- rshepherdfloraldesign.com
- ryeworkshop.com
- www.sincerelypete.com/
- thattimeevents.com

## Entertainment

- azlyrics.com/
- djkeelez.com
- gigmasters.com/services/wedding-dj
- spotify.com/us/
- weddingvendors.com/music/

## Jewelry

- adorn.com
- bario-neal.com
- bluenile.com
- cartier.us
- catbirdnyc.com
- clay-pot.com
- jared.com
- rehsdiamonds.com
- Swarovski.com

## LGBT

- asta.org
- gayweddings.com/vendors

- rainbowweddingnetwork.com
- theknot.com/gay-lesbian-weddings

## Photography and videography

- alanphillip.com
- chelseamasonphotography.com
- heatherwaraksa.com
- lollievideography.com
- michellelytle.com
- studioten9ten.com/

## Stationary and paper goods

- etsy.com
- invitations.davidsbridal.com
- marissaalliedesigns.com
- minted.com
- moontreeletterpress.com
- sesameletterpress.com
- paperlesspost.com
- papersource.com
- papyrusonline.com
- weddingpaperdivas.com
- zazzle.com

## Travel

- airbnb.com
- asta.org
- carrentals.com
- destinationweddings.com
- expedia.com
- iglta.org
- theknot.com
- vrbo.com

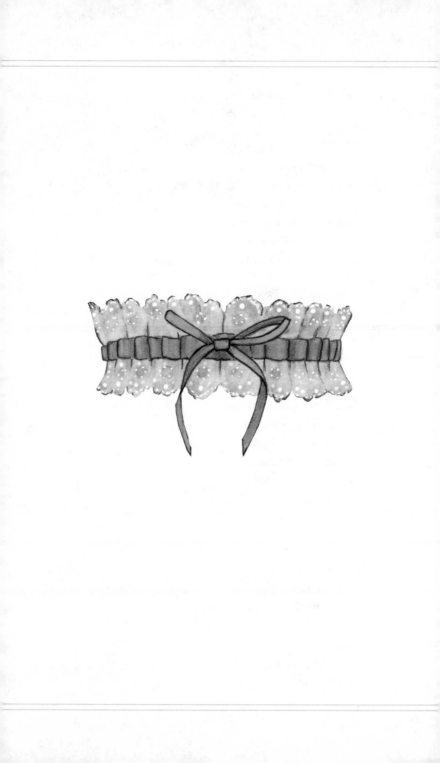